Outlaws

In The

Big

Thicket

By Wanda A. Landrey

Illustrated by Thelma Hardy

Published in the United States of America
By Nortex Press, P.O. Box 120, Quanah, Texas 79252

Library of Congress Catalogue Card No. 76-555-16

ISBN 0-89015-144-X

This book is gratefully dedicated to my friend, Lois Williams Parker, director of reserve reading at Lamar University, whose knowledge, as a native of the Big Thicket, years of careful research, and continous service to the Big Thicket Association and Museum, have contributed greatly to preserving the rich historical and natural heritage of this unique area of Texas.

A TYPICAL Thicket woods scene

(Roy Hamric - photographer)

FOREWORD

The Big Thicket of Texas, lying north and northwest of Beaumont, northward to the Old Spanish Road (that ran from Nacogdoches to San Antonio), and extending from the Sabine River on the east to westward of the Trinity on the west, covered about three and one-half million acres of land when the first Europeans arrived. This had been cut back to about one and one-half million acres by the 1930's, and probably less than 300,000 acres remain today, less than one-tenth of its original size. This remnant is scattered in bits and pieces, primarily in Hardin, Liberty, Polk, Tyler, Newton, Jasper and Jefferson Counties.

Wanda Landrey's Preface and other descriptive passages in her interesting study of lawlessness in the Big Thicket give an idea of its richness of plant life, where outlaws hid. Its varied and diverse soils, with its mild Gulf climate and sixty inches of rainfall a year, have made the Big Thicket an area of lush and unique plant life, sheltering a very rich bird and reptile life, and, until hunted out, a rich mammal life.

The Big Thicket is a very unusual region of critical species change, and is often called the "biological cross-roads of North America," because it is a "meeting and mixing place for the flora and fauna of North and South, East and West." The largest existing of eleven different species of American trees are found in the Big Thicket, as well as four out of five of the American plants that catch and eat insects.

It is an area of tall blooming magnolias, of wild peach trees, of scented bay trees, of great oaks draped with Spanish moss, of clinging vines and small shrubs, and many wild flowers; of sloughs and swamps, baygalls and palmetto groves, creeks and small ponds, and all the animal, fish, reptile,

7

A THICKET CHURCH

(Roy Hamric - photographer)

and insect life that you would expect to find in such an area.

For the lawless, the Big Thicket offered the best natural hiding place in Texas. It also offered more than a hiding place; it contained food for survival. Wild game, wild nuts and fruit were there in abundance. Hickory nuts, black walnuts, acorns and chinquapins could be collected and stored, while plum thickets varied from spring plums to summer plums, with persimmons in the fall. There were black berries and dewberries, black haws and red haws, mayhaws and huckleberries; grapes: spring grapes, summer grapes, fall grapes, 'possum grapes, mustang grapes, muscadines and scuppernongs, and other fruit, nuts and plant food to be found in the woods, meadows, swamps, and stream margins.

While the plant food was abundant, the lawless among the human inhabitants, unlike the settlers with families in the Thicket, probably relied little upon it, but went for meat for survival. Located in the Mississippi Flyway, ducks were abundant from fall to spring, with geese on the Neches River, but the greatest availability was in non-migratory game: deer and turkey, squirrels, raccoons, 'possum, and quail, the latter trapped by the covey without the use of expensive powder and lead.

The two great sources of food supply for the lawless or the fugitives, as well as the settler, are yet to be mentioned: bear and hog meat. The Thicket was a natural home and one of the last Texas refuges of the American black bear. Hogs left the makeshift pens of the early settlers, and roamed in abundant numbers in the Thicket, a "hog heaven." The East Texas razorback was an intelligent, resourceful animal in the wild, but nevertheless became a main source of food to man and bear. This new source of food greatly enlarged the bear population. With a hog or a bear for camp food, people in the Thicket

CREEK SCENES

(Courtesy - Fisher Collection - Lamar University)

10

did not need to spend all their hours seeking food from woods and stream.

Frank Dobie narrates how Ben Lilly, hunter, had killed more than a hundred bear in the Thicket, and there were others whose total passed the century mark; Uncle Bud Brackin claimed to have killed 305 Big Thicket bears. These records were made by hunters or settlers, not by outlaws, fugitives from the law, or criminals.

Americans are fascinated by the lives of outlaws, but the majority of the people in the Thicket, like the majority outside, were basically law abiding people, except where game laws were involved — the latter were viewed as a drinking man viewed prohibition.

The law abiding majority of people in the Thicket came to the Wilderness for their own way of life — like Daniel Boone, they did not care to be close enough to neighbors to see the smoke of their chimneys.

Dozens of books have been written about the Thicket, and hundreds of monographs, magazines and newspaper articles. It was first vividly described in books in the first half of the 1800's. People lived in the Thicket, some as wild as the animals they hunted.

Out of this storied area have come books of the folklore and legends of the Big Thicket, books about its flora and fauna, and geological formations. Dramas have been written and produced about its history; poems have been penned and songs written and sung about it. Nature trails and museums give a taste of its color even yet. The lawless and the law enforcing left their marks too — but the basic food and shelter made this area of beauty and light a cover up place for dark deeds also.

The Big Thicket has a large niche in the history of how people lived in the woodlands of the East. Not all legends are about outlawery; there are other fabled legends, many collected in Dr. Francis Aber-

11

PALMETTO FERNS and Spanish moss

nethy's book, *Tales from the Big Thicket*. The lights on the Ghost Road are as real to the people of the Big Thicket as the real Hangman's Noose was for the wayward highwayman.

Such a wonderland of beautiful plant life and interesting animal life, the former home of the exotic Ivory-billed Woodpecker, and present home of the endangered Texas Red Wolf and the Red-cockaded Woodpecker, would naturally interest conservationists, earth scientists and naturalists in the preservation of a part of the Thicket. In the 1930's, a Big Thicket Association was formed, and a Park of about 400,000 acres was proposed and virtually agreed upon (about 1 1/2 million acres of the Thicket still remained then), but the intervention of World War II stopped action upon the plan, and the chemical discovery of making pulp paper out of pine trees led to the rapid proliferation of pulp pine plantations, and made the Big Thicket itself an endangered species.

In the 1960's, proposals for either a State or a National Park were advanced, as the rapid bulldozing away of the natural Big Thicket plant life, to make way for more pine plantations, spurred the scientific community, the conservationists, and the naturalists, into a race against time and the bulldozers, to save a remnant of the once vast Big Thicket.

Efforts to create a State Big Thicket Park failed in the 1960's; I introduced a Big Thicket Park Bill in the U.S. Senate in 1966; my Big Thicket National Park Bill, for a 100,000 acre Park, passed the Senate in 1970, but failed in the House. The Big Thicket Association, ably led by Dr. Pete Gunter and Maxine Johnston, their work buttressed by the great knowledge of the Thicket of the late Lance Rosier "Mr. Big Thicket," and Geraldine Watson, and aided by The Sierra Club and many other conservation-minded organizations, worked to push to passage in the Congress in 1974 a Big Thicket National Biological Reserve Bill of 84,550 acres. It re-

13

BIG THICKET PALMETTOS

(Courtesy - Fisher Collection - Lamar University.)

14

sulted from a compromise worked out by Congressmen Charles Wilson and Robert Eckhardt of Texas. Congress passed the bill, but failed to appropriate the money to buy these choice shreds of the once great blanket of foliage that lay upon the earth. The fight to save this portion of the Thicket still goes on, as of this writing in 1976, while timber cutting continues in these 84,550 acres. Congress has finally appropriated this year over twenty-three million dollars to buy areas in immediate danger of being cut, and the Army Engineers and National Park Officials are in a diligent race with time and the saws and bulldozers to save these treasure spots. Thousands of acres have been cut, but by October 1st, 4800 acres will have been bought by the Park Service, and it is estimated that 38,000 acres will have been purchased and saved by October, 1977. An attempt to create a drainage district was pushed in the Commissioners Court of Hardin County and in the Legislature of Texas in 1975, to ditch and drain a sizeable part of this small segment of the Thicket surveyed for salvation. It failed in 1975, but it is rumored that the forces of destruction will try again in 1977.

The Age of Lawlessness of man toward man in the Big Thicket is over, but greedy man still wages war upon this treasured heritage of all Americans in these little natural wonderland areas left.

I wonder if the Supreme Being who sees even a sparrow fall may not view the destruction of this natural cover and blanket of the land and, protected by it, all its living creatures (other than man) placed there by Providence, this crime against defenseless nature, as a greater lawlessness than the lawlessness that men once practiced against each other here.

With Arch Fullingim and 97 year old Mrs. Hill, 'Ma Thicket," and those other writers whose pen and paper have carried forward the battle to save the Big Thicket for over forty years, let us resolve

LOGGING OPERATIONS
Virgin Loblolly trees-average age over 200 years

(Courtesy - Fisher Collection - Lamar University)

that our efforts will not lessen, that this part of the Thicket must and will be saved. Let the lawlessness against nature go the way of lawlessness of man against man. We relegate both to a primitive society which we Texans should long ago have outgrown.

Ralph W. Yarborough,

President
Big Thicket Association

LOGGING OPERATIONS of the 1940's

(Courtesy - Fisher Collection - Lamar University Library)

17

EXAMPLE OF a turn of the century Thicket cabin.

(Roy Hamric - photographer)

CUT AND SHOOT, a community in Montgomery County on the outskirts of the Big Thicket, derives its name from an argument which resulted among area residents over the design of a church steeple.

18

PREFACE

Just as it is possible for crime to develop from accident, whim, lack of law and order, logic or character of the people, so, too, can geography play a significant role. Such can be said of one of the most unusual geographical areas in the United States, the well-known Big Thicket of East Texas.

I think I have always been fascinated by the Big Thicket. Being a descendant of an early East Texas family and having relatives living in the Thicket, I had many occasions as a child to view the land at first-hand. This was before there was any big movement to make the lush subtropical forest into a national park. Then the Big Thicket was known only to a relatively small number of people — naturalists, historians, scientists, hunters, and some hardy pioneer types whose ancestors were the original settlers.

My first interest in the area was not with the exotic flora and fauna, but with the intriguing stories of crimes which had taken place within its depths. I can remember asking my father, T.L. Cruse, many times to give me a step by step account of the Sapp murders, and each time he complied with every version becoming a little more vivid and much gorier. Soon this story along with the episodes of the Kaiser Burnout and the escapades of "Red" Goleman took precedence over his usual bedtime stories such as "Goldilocks" and "Little Red Riding Hood."

My somewhat distorted first impression of the Big Thicket as being an outlaw haven naturally changed with maturity. I began to realize that crime was no more prevalent here than in other isolated areas like the early period in the Texas Panhandle and in the lands along the Rio Grande. And for the most part Big Thicket inhabitants have always been law abiding, even though in the earlier days the only law existing was their own. Nevertheless, through the years the Big Thicket served the outlaw longer than most other isolated places in our country by providing him with the seclusion he desired. Geography may not cause a man to become an outlaw type, but it aids him by supplying him with an environment conducive to crime. To me this has been the role that the Big Thicket played in its lawlessness.

The Indians along the Gulf Coast, the Tonkawas and the Karankawas, called the Thicket "Big Woods," and later the early Anglo-American pioneers gave it the name "Big Thicket." The area was aptly named because it contains some of the densest woodlands found anywhere in America. In spite of the vast destruction long dealt the land by avarice and apathy, virgin sections remain unmarred by human hands. Many places entangled with trees, vines, and undergrowth give the Thicket a junglelike appearance, and make it almost impossible to penetrate. The most experienced outdoorsman enters this jungle with caution, aware that its depths can play tricks and that he can easily be fooled into losing his way. He is also wary of falling into one of the many pits of Thicket quicksand which are well disguised by several layers of crusty soil. Spanning approximately fifty miles in length and covering all of Hardin and parts of Liberty, Polk, and Tyler counties, the Big Thicket remains one of our country's last frontiers.

Through the years the Thicket has acted as a barrier against encroaching modern civilization, and, as a result, this isolation has kept alive in its inhabitants many pioneer modes of living. For example, such items as the cook stove, the glass windowpane, and the sewing machine did not appear in the area until long after the Civil War. And even today, according to Stanley Coe, former District Attorney of Hardin County, the clock is not always considered a necessity. Only recently while hunting in the Thicket, Coe spotted an old cabin with a well nearby. Being thirsty, he ventured closer and asked a woman sitting in a rocking chair on the rickety porch for a drink of water. After a few cordial words and a cool drink from the well, Coe asked the woman for the time. Rocking back and forth at the same steady pace, the woman looked up at the sunlight shining through a hole in the roof, then quickly down to the floor and replied, "Why, it's two cracks 'til twelve."

Many Thicket people feel that the ways of their ancestors are better than those of modern times. Right after the close of World War I a civil engineering party was surveying the right-of-way for Highway 105 which, when finished, led through a dense part of the Big Thicket. One particular morning men in the crew found their way blocked by an elderly woman who was riding bareback on a gray mule with a shotgun across her lap. As they started to work, the woman raised the gun, cocked it, and pointed it toward the men. "Don't you come no further. The fust one of you that sets a foot past that stump there gits his head blowed off." The young engineers didn't argue but by-passed the old woman's property and took up the survey on the other side of her little farm.

The same feeling still exists among some of the Big Thicketeers. Only recently a party laying a high power line through the Thicket area found the right-of-way survey lay directly over the middle of an old Negro's log cabin. The old man steadfastly refused to accept pay for his property and move off the right-of-way, so the company completed their construction and the line now runs across the middle of the house.

Isolation also caused some of the settlers to become accustomed to acting on their own when it came to law and order. Many of these inhabitants have long regarded making homebrew and killing game, in season and out, as a way of providing food and drink for their families. Of course, they were

not averse to selling their products to those they regarded as close-mouthed enough to keep their secrets. The law has often not only been disregarded, but, until recent years, has been hampered by insufficient funds needed to afford men, transportation, and communication devices necessary to provide effective law enforcement.

Furthermore, in addition to the natives making their own rules, the very nature of the Thicket attracted a segment of the outlaws from outside its borders. Its denseness, coupled with its abundance of food and game, has made it an ideal place in which to commit a crime or to hide until trouble committed elsewhere blew over.

Much has been written preserving the history of the Big Thicket but the subject of lawlessness, so far as I know, has been left to widely talked about stories and tales, often varying in accuracy from true facts.

In the following chapters, various episodes of lawlessness and records of more serious crimes in the Big Thicket have been presented. This book does not claim to be a complete record of lawlessness in the area, but the stories in it have been verified and authenticated whenever possible with the hope of giving an accurate and, hopefully, interesting picture of an important part of the history of the Big Thicket of East Texas.

ACKNOWLEDGMENTS

My sincerest thanks go to Mrs. Lois Williams Parker of the Lamar University Library. Mrs. Parker not only shared with me her excellent source of collected materials and her wealth of knowledge about the Big Thicket, but also gave freely of her time throughout the research and writing of this manuscript. For these things I am most grateful.

Special appreciation goes to: Lamar University Professors Ralph Wooster, Wesley Norton, Adrian N. Anderson, and John Ellis for their very helpful advisement; Miss Alice Cashen and Mrs. Ruth Garrison Scurlock for their valuable editorial services; Mr. James A. Clark of Houston for giving me access to articles written by him and others; my aunt, Mrs. Ila Sanders, for her aid in arranging various interviews in Hardin County; my husband, Mr. Floyd Landrey, for rendering his legal assistance; and Mrs. Estelle Suess for the typing of the manuscript.

I wish to also thank the following people who were very interested and willing: Mr. Dee Barfield, Beaumont Police Chief Willie Bauer, the late Mr. A.L. Bevil, Dr. John Bevil, Dr. George Beto, Mr. W.T. Block, the late Miss Mittye Bradley, Mrs. Carlyse Bliss Brechin, Mr. O.P. Brown, the late Mr. W.H. "Billy" Bryant, Mrs. W.B. Cariker, Mr. Hugh Clubb, Mr. Joe Combs, the late Mr. B.L. Cornwell, Mrs. B.L. Cornwell, the late Mr. Lark Cornwell, Mrs. T.L. Cruse, Mr. E.D. Edmonson, Mrs. Addie Ewing, Mrs. Homer French, Mr. A.J. Guedry, Mr. Archer Fullingim, Dr. A.Y. Gunter, Mr. Roy Hamric, Mr. Bob Hubert, the late Mr. M.H. Johnston, Miss Maxine Johnston and the staff of the Lamar Library, Dr. Russell Long, Mr. O.H. Matthews, Mr. James A. Moye, Mrs. Violette Newton, the late Mr. Henry Overstreet, Estell Parrish of the Corrigan-Camden Independent School District, Hardin County Sheriff Billy Paine, Mr. L.M. Phillips, Mr. William Quick, Mr. Cooper K. Ragan, Mr. J.P. Richardson, the late Mrs. J.P. Richardson, the late Mr. Lance Rossier, Mr. Cecil Sapp, Mr. Milton Turner, the late Mrs. Hazel Hilliard Waters, Mrs. Carmen Watley, the late Mrs. Ada Lee Williams, Mrs. Gwendolyn Wingate, and the Hon. Ralph W. Yarborough.

In conclusion, I wish to acknowledge my indebtedness to my father, the late Mr. T.L. Cruse, whose stories of the Big Thicket held me spellbound in my childhood.

CABIN in the Thicket

TABLE OF CONTENTS

CHAPTER I

Murders in the

Bay Galls

When the subject of Big Thicket crimes is mentioned to any long-time resident of Southeast Texas, the conversation turns to a series of murders which occurred in the second decade of the twentieth century. These murders — events leading to them and the solution of the crimes — form an almost incredible story easily comparable to anything a fiction writer with the wildest imagination might envision. The old adage "Truth is stranger than fiction" was never more applicable.

The story begins with the early part of February, 1915, in one of the densest places in the Thicket. A farmer, L.P. Wright, and his son who were hunting near their home noticed buzzards flying overhead. Thinking that perhaps one of their cattle had died, the pair decided to investigate. One can imagine their horror when they parted the dense undergrowth and saw, instead of a dead animal, the body of a man half buried in a shallow grave and partially eaten by the birds. Wright quickly notified Hardin County officers of their terrible find and guided officers to the grave. After examining the corpse, the officials reported that the man had been dead for approximately two weeks from bullet wounds in his chest. Other officers were called in and a more thorough investigation was made.

Identification of the corpse as Richard Watts, an oil field worker, came from a Beaumont dentist, Dr.

---

* Low, marshy, and densely grown spots found throughout the Big Thicket.

29

J.P. Evans, who, not long before, had done some unusual dental work on Watts. The extracted teeth from the deceased matched Dr. Evans' work. Further identity was established when Sam Bishop, a cousin of Richard Watts, recognized the clothing of the dead man.

Although many theories developed as to the motive for the crime, it was not until more than a month later that any arrests were made. On March 13, warrants were issued in Hardin County for the arrests of two well-known Beaumonters, Emory Eran Sapp and his younger half-brother, Louis Sapp. A preliminary hearing soon followed in Kountze, county seat of Hardin County, where testimonies were taken to be presented to the grand jury.

While awaiting further legal action, another startling thing occurred. Frank Havard, a friend of Richard Watts, was reported missing. Since Havard had not appeared at the preliminary hearing as an important witness, one of the prosecuting attorneys, W.R. Blain, concluded that Havard might have been murdered, also. Blain organized a searching party, composed of Wright, his son, and two others. With shovels, a wagon, and a team, the group went to the spot in the Thicket where Watts had been found and started a systematic search from that point. It was not long before they came upon what they expected — the body of Frank Havard. Buried in a similar shallow grave and only seventy feet from the grave of Richard Watts, the body showed a bullet wound in the head. Several days later the grand jury indicted the Sapp brothers on the charge of murdering both Richard Watts and Frank Havard.

On April 29, the habeas corpus hearing in the case of Watts began in Kountze to show cause why the defendants should not be released on bail. Judge J. Llewellyn presided, substituting for Judge L.B. Hightower of the Ninth District Court. From

E.E. SAPP   LOU SAPP

PICTURES OF E.E. SAPP and Lou Sapp appeared in the *Beaumont Journal* on March 28, 1918, shortly after E.E. Sapp was sentenced to ninety-nine years in the state penitentiary. One of the victims they were charged with murdering was Frank Harvard.

FRANK HARVARD

31

start to finish interest ran high. Old-timers recall that never before or since have there been as many people in the small town. Farmers and their wives came in wagons and on horseback, and business and professional men traveled from the nearby cities. People arrived early each morning hoping to secure the best seats in the courtroom. When court adjourned at noon each day, the courtyard resembled a big old-fashioned picnic with many of the local youths taking advantage of the situation by selling pop-corn and soda pop. The hotel and boarding house proprietors also did a thriving business. Not to turn away customers when all the rooms were rented, the hotel owners quickly put up cots and pallets in the halls.

The curious spectators rushed to the courthouse the first morning of the trial, all eager to get a good look at the defendants. Louis Sapp, a giant of a man, towered over everyone from his height of six feet, five inches. He was about twenty years old, much younger than his brother. At the time of his arrest, he had been employed as a fireman in Beaumont. E.E. Sapp, in his middle thirties, was described as being most affable and handsome. He had dark eyes, black hair, and was about six feet tall. Having had little schooling, he worked most of his life as a common laborer. However, for several years prior to his arrest, he had served in various capacities as a law enforcement officer.

Nine months before, on July 12, 1914, Em, as the older brother was often called, married an elderly woman of considerable wealth by the name of Mrs. Ellen E. Partain. While out on a hunting trip the following autumn, she had been shot and killed. It was around this event that the prosecution based its case. Throughout the hearing, the State tried to prove that Em married the older woman for her money. The State alleged that Sapp hired someone to kill her after convincing her to will him all her property. According to the prosecution, Sapp first approached Frank Havard but Havard refused his offer. The job was later accepted by Richard Watts. The ill-fated hunting party, composed of E.E. Sapp, his wife, Frank Havard, Richard Watts, and several others, camped near the Trinity River close to the town of Romayor in Liberty County. Although it had first been reported that Watts accidentally shot Mrs. Sapp while cleaning his gun, the State contended that it had been premeditated murder. The crime was obviously preying on Richard Watts' conscience, and he began telling friends that he had been hired by Sapp to kill his wife. The State further alleged that it was then that E.E. Sapp and his brother, Louis, took Watts into the Thicket about five miles south of the town of Nona between Kountze and Sour Lake and killed him. When the two brothers heard that Frank Havard was also talking too much, they decided to eliminate any possible chance of detection and subsequently murdered him.

The defense admitted no part of the State's theory, except that E.E. Sapp married an elderly woman. On May 8, the hearing ended with the court ruling that the defendants be remanded to jail without bail to await further trial. Soon after, troubles mounted even more for Em Sapp. The grand jury in Liberty County, the county where Mrs. Sapp was killed, indicted him on charges of her murder.

During the summer months, the Sapp brothers remained in the Hardin County jail awaiting further legal action. Meanwhile some enterprising person or persons wrote an account of the Sapp case and sent it to Chicago to be published. The following article, which appeared in a local newspaper at the time, made reference to the account:

The Sapp Grave Yard

The book would have been off the press on July 1st, but we seen [sic] it would be so in complete [sic], and decided to wait on some later developments in the case which will make up the last chapters of the book.

There was a reward offered for a suitable name for the book, and after considering 82 names by 89 different people, it has been decided to use the above name. Books will be delivered this fall.

Another article relating to the book appeared in the same newspaper at a later date:

The Sapp Grave Yard Book is ready for delivery, but owing to a miss under standing [sic] with the publisher in Chicago, the 1st shipment of 2000 books are being held for a payment of $150.00. If those who subscribed for a book will send in the dollar, we can deliver them in two weeks. We guarantee satisfaction or refund your money.

The sum of money was apparently never fully collected because no evidence was found that the publishers ever released the copies of the book.

The following September, attorneys for the defense asked for a change of venue in the Richard Watts case on grounds that prejudice existed against the two men in Hardin County. The application was granted and the case was transferred to Jasper County, the nearest county not subject to the same objections. Later another change of venue was granted, and the proceedings went to Lufkin in Angelina County.

After several delays, the legal battle commenced again on May 2, 1916. By then, the unusual circumstances surrounding the trial caused interest to spread throughout the state and it became known as the famous "Sapp Case." Just as people were drawn to the previous habeas corpus hearing in Kountze, spectators thronged to the Second District Courtroom of Angelina County.

Although the Sapp brothers were on trial in Lufkin for the murder of Richard Watts, the close relationship of the alleged murders of Em Sapp's wife and Frank Havard caused both the State and the defense to introduce evidence connected with their deaths. During the opening speeches, the State, basing its charge on circumstantial evidence, told of its plans to try to prove its previously mentioned allegations. The defense, led by C.W. Howth, gave a lengthy account of its plans. Howth declared that the defense would show that:

> ... E.E. Sapp was a game warden and had been sent to Matagorda County to apprehend some citizen who had discovered the old Indian art of calling deer; that it was in the late fall of 1913 or early spring of 1914 when he first met the lady he married; that the couple frequently went on hunting trips together. The State contends Sapp induced his wife to make her will in his favor. We will show that the will was not only freely and willingly made, but that Mrs. Sapp offered to give her husband the balance of what she possessed. We will show that at the time of the death of Mrs. Sapp the whole party had planned to break camp and leave the day before, but that out of deference to the wishes of Mrs. Sapp they refrained another day, showing the matter was not prearranged. If the hunting trip had, as a matter of fact, been carried out as E.E. Sapp planned it, Mrs. Sapp would doubtless be alive today. We will also show that as long as Watts and Havard were alive

Sapp was secure from prosecution. We will show that Sapp knew that he was constantly being watched by his wife's relatives and private prosecution from the time of her death, and knowing that he was watched, would not have committed such an act, selecting a road frequently traveled by him.

It became apparent in the Lufkin trial that Em Sapp did not agree with the idea that the criminal who travels alone travels farthest. Testimony showed that many people were involved in the alleged murders. All in all, more than four hundred witnesses were summoned, of whom one hundred were placed on the stand.

During the trial, the State attempted to prove that a conspiracy existed as far back as 1912. A witness testified that he was in Beaumont one day that year and visited with Em Sapp and Thomas Van Auken in the latter's jewelry store. Van Auken told the witness that he knew about an elderly, rich widow he could marry. He stated that Van Auken mentioned something about eliminating her and dividing the money among the three of them. During the conversation, the witness contended that Sapp said that he would marry the woman himself if he were not already married. The State then offered as evidence the petition for divorce filed by E.E. Sapp against Minnie Sapp in the District Court at Jasper on March 28, 1913.

Next, the prosecution introduced in evidence the wedding invitation announcing the marriage of E.E. Sapp and Mrs. Ellen E. Partain in the Thomas Van Auken home on July 12, 1914. Trying further to prove that money was the basis for the marriage, the State presented a bank ledger showing that $19,500.00 was deposited in the account of E.E. Sapp only six days after the marriage took place.

Another State witness described how unhappy

the new Mrs. Sapp was after their marriage. Seldom were Em and his bride seen together, and that soon after the marriage, Sapp bought an automobile and was often seen driving young women around town.

The prosecution later brought Richard Watts and Frank Havard into the alleged conspiracy. Liquor has been said to be the downfall of many a man and from the statements of several State witnesses, this axiom applied to Watts and Havard. Their elimination may have become necessary because they were both susceptible to alcohol and when intoxicated, made statements saying they could get money from Sapp and why. It was the contention of the State that their fatal journey into the Big Thicket was made after the Sapps had succeeded in getting them drunk.

Finally, the State attempted to prove by circumstantial evidence the events which would link the Sapp brothers to the actual killings of Watts and Havard. Therefore, the prosecution had to trace the so called "death marches" from Beaumont to the actual location of the killings. Witnesses testified that on the morning of January 7, 1915, Dick Watts, Frank Havard, and the Sapp brothers were together at a Beaumont saloon across the street from the Santa Fe depot. E.E. Sapp left in his automobile shortly before train time and Louis Sapp and Watts boarded the train. Three other witnesses stated that on the same day they noticed a big man, who was apparently drunk and was assisted by a younger man, get off the train at Lumberton, enter a waiting black car, and drive off towards the Big Thicket. Another witness told the court that he heard rifle shots near the place where Watts was found, and others reported seeing the two Sapp brothers leaving the Thicket the same day. One feminine witness stated that she had seen the Sapps passing her home going toward Beaumont early in January. When the State asked if the vehicle she had seen was an automobile, she replied quickly, "No, Judge, it was a Ford." Witnesses alleged that Frank Havard was later killed in the same manner as Richard Watts.

After offering fifty-six witnesses and arguing that the links in the chain of circumstantial evidence were sufficient to convict the Sapp brothers, the counsel for the State closed its side of the case.

Immediately, the defense began calling its witnesses, doing everything possible to refute the testimonies presented by the State and attempting, also, to develop a theory of its own. It put on a mass of evidence to establish an alibi for the defendants.

More than three weeks of tedious evidence was heard by both the State and the defense before the case was presented to the jury for final judging. Along with all the detailed evidence, the testimony of one relatively unimportant witness served as comic relief from the gruelling days of questioning. The witness was a Beaumont newspaper reporter who had interviewed members of the Big Thicket hunting party after they returned with the body of Mrs. Sapp in 1914. The newspaperman told the jury that during this interview, Em Sapp appeared very upset and frequently cried. One minor question that the reporter asked was, "Mr. Sapp, was any big game killed by anyone on the hunt?" Sapp looked intently at the man for a moment, took out his handkerchief and loudly blew his nose, then replied, "No, there was no big game killed."

After deliberating for eighty-two hours, the jurymen returned their verdict. They found both defendants guilty of murder and assessed the punishments at forty years confinement in the state penitentiary for E.E. Sapp and twenty years in the state penitentiary for Louis Sapp.

Attorneys for the defendants immediately appealed the case to the Court of Criminal Appeals in Austin. Finding the trial court in error on several counts, the appellate court called for a new trial.

During the next two years the Sapp murder case was tossed about like a ball, transferred from one Texas court to another. Several months after the trial in Lufkin, legal proceedings began again against E.E. Sapp for the murder of his wife. After numerous delays, Sapp was tried at Bryan in March, 1918. He was found guilty and sentenced to ninety-nine years in the state penitentiary.

As in the Watts case, the attorneys for the defense appealed the case to Austin, but this time the Court of Criminal Appeals agreed with the Bryan court and the verdict was affirmed.

While these legal proceedings were being instituted against E.E. Sapp, the reversed Watts case **was transferred from Lufkin to Waxahachie for** trial. The following months offered nothing but confinement for Lou Sapp while various preliminary hearings kept the case from being tried. Finally, in June, 1919, more than a year after his older brother was convicted in Bryan, Lou was released from jail on a $7,000 bond. In November of 1935, Lou Sapp made news again when it was reported that he surrendered to officers in Louisiana for the slaying of a patient in a hospital in New Orleans.

Emory Eran Sapp entered the Texas Department of Corrections on July 13, 1920. In prison he conducted himself like a man who had learned the futility of defying the law. He was quiet and obedient, exemplifying a model prisoner. As a result of his excellent behavior, he was transferred to the Eastham prison farm where he soon became a "trusty" and was given numerous privileges.

On April 11, 1930, after ten years on the farm, the prisoner mentioned that he was going fishing. Since Sapp had often taken fishing trips, no one refused him the privilege, so he climbed into a boat and shoved off into the river which bordered the farm.

That was the last that the Eastham prison farm

saw of Em Sapp. The boat was later found bottom-side up, and not far away were the convict's shoes and hat. Officials ruled that Sapp had either drowned purposely or accidentally while trying to escape. What the authorities did not know was that Sapp only made it appear that he had met his death and simply walked away.

After escaping from prison, Em Sapp settled in Johnson City, Tennessee, where he assumed the name of a deceased brother, Thomas H. Sapp, a Spanish-American veteran. There he married, had three children, and became a respected citizen serving as a member of the police department.

But one day in November, 1940, the wheel of fate brought Em Sapp's smoothly-running life to an abrupt halt. Two years earlier after a federal law was passed enabling the widows of Spanish-American War veterans to become eligible for pensions, the widow of the real Thomas H. Sapp applied for an annuity. The federal government, of course, had begun an investigation when it discovered that a person by that name had been collecting veteran's compensation for years. It was inevitable that the truth about the past of the escaped "lifer" would soon come to light.

On March 4, 1941, a federal court sentenced Em Sapp to ten years' imprisonment and fined him $4,800 on the pension fraud conviction. This sentence, however, was held in abeyance, ready to be carried out if the ex-policeman should win parole or pardon in Texas.

E.E. Sapp was returned to the Texas prison in Huntsville on March 19 where he resumed the eighty-nine years left of his sentence. Soon after his return, he appeared on a nation-wide broadcast and told his amazing story. Sympathizers responded en masse by sending him letters of encouragement and also by writing Coke Stevenson, then governor of Texas, begging for Sapp's freedom. The appeals were not made in vain for on December 22, 1943,

Governor Stevenson granted Sapp a conditional pardon to the Federal authorities. He returned to Tennessee where he had been convicted of the pension fraud and was sent to the United States Penitentiary at Leavenworth, Kansas, on January 23, 1944. He served about fourteen months on that sentence and was granted a conditional release. He returned to Johnson City and again worked as a police officer. Little was heard of his activities for several years.

Archer Fullingim, former editor of the *Kountze News,* often printed a one-line sentence in his weekly newspaper which was of interest to his reading public. In the early part of 1955, the Kountze newspaper ran the question, "Remember 'Em' Sapp?" Several weeks later the citizens of Kountze could hardly believe it when E.E. Sapp appeared in town. Most people accused Fullingim of having some information regarding Sapp or, perhaps, of being clairvoyant. According to the editor, he printed the question only as a passing thought and as an interesting item to help fill the front page.

At seventy-seven years of age, Em Sapp was described as resembling a minister more than the notorious character that he was. He was a well-preserved, immaculately dressed man with the same pleasing manner he had exhibited thirty-nine years earlier. For the next few years Sapp lived most of the time in Silsbee, where he was employed as a night watchman.

But Em Sapp and the law were not through feuding. In May, 1962, Sapp was arrested in Silsbee as a parole violator as a result of his buying and carrying a gun off duty. On June 30, 1962, he was again returned to the state penitentiary. He died on March 12, 1963, less than a year later, at the age of eighty-five in the prison hospital in Huntsville. His cause of death was diagnosed as a hypertensive cardiovascular disease. Unclaimed by any relatives or friends, he was buried in the prison cemetery at Huntsville.

During his later years, Sapp professed never to have had a care in his life. While this may have been true for him, it did not hold true for his innocent relatives who have since tried to live down the unsavory reputation he built. Cecil Sapp, an amiable gentleman living in Sabine Pass, tells about how, as a nephew, he had many a childhood fight just because his name was Sapp. Most Sapp relatives, however, are simply reluctant to talk. They take no pride whatever in being kin to one of the most sensational characters ever to be tried in a Texas court of law.

Publicity given the Sapp case kept the Big Thicket in the public eye for many years and added to the idea that the Thicket was a dark and sinister place where danger lurked in each bay gall.

BIG THICKET BAYGALL

The base of the trees have been permanently discolored from water which often stands here.

CHAPTER II

Mysteries

from the past

During the early part of 1967 in the northern part of the Big Thicket woods, a giant beech tree was felled by a logging contractor and hauled to a lumber mill in the nearby town of Batson. There the huge log was put in line to go through the mill. The night before it was scheduled to be sawed into lumber, a night watchman spotted interesting carvings cut deep into its bark. He revealed his discovery to the mill owner the next morning and the log was pulled back in an attempt to decipher the carvings. The two men noticed pictures as well as writings.

The carvings showed a hanging tree with the body of a man dangling at the end of a rope. Below the figure were dates, either 1809-38 or 1803-38, indicating that the carvings undoubtedly took place while Texas was a republic. To the right of the hanging man were pictures of several teepees, presumably an Indian village, and the carving of a man wearing an elaborate headdress, apparently an Indian chief. Near him was a down-turned arrow. While many persons have speculated on the meaning of these carvings, no one has yet solved this clue to the past. The answer, like much of the early history of the Big Thicket, was forgotten years ago.

Residents of the area are equally intrigued about the numerous legends relating to the "Saratoga Light," seen often by travelers passing along the Old Bragg road, an old tram road in the midst of the Thicket. Oldtimers, in particular, refuse to accept the logical explanation of scientists that the

LOOKING north on the   Ghost Road

(Roy Hamric - photographer)

44

luminous ball is caused from gaseous substances arising from the swamps of the surrounding woods. These persons have their own interesting, but not so logical, opinions. Some contend that the "light" often shines over a treasure buried in the woods by early Spanish conquistadors who failed to return for it, others say it is the remains of the fire that was never completely extinguished after the famous Kaiser Burnout of Civil War days. Some of the most imaginative get a little more gruesome and say that the fiery ball is the ghostly light of Mexican crewmen who are supposedly buried near the one-time railroad line. They say that the Mexicans, hired to help cut the right-of-way and lay the tracks, were murdered by the foreman of the road gang who refused to pay them a large sum of accumulated wages. Their souls continually haunt the land that cost them their lives.

These are only a few of the legendary tales of crimes circulating around the Big Thicket nowadays. As in many areas, accounts of the Thicket's history often rely heavily on handed-down stories because few early records were preserved. Nevertheless, the few existing records, along with the less reliable sources, provide a basis for study which contributes greatly to a better understanding of the lives of the people who lived in the Thicket area in the earliest days of its settlement.

EUROPEAN EXPLORATIONS

Available records trace the history of the Big Thicket back to the period of the European explorations which began in the late 1600's. While it is doubtful that any Spanish or French adventurers penetrated the area, it was known that they traveled along its borders. According to the early historian Henderson Yoakum, the French explorer, La Salle, was among the first. After being granted permission by his king, Louis XIV, to establish a colony at the mouth of the Mississippi River, La Salle sailed from France on July 24, 1684, taking with him 280 persons, including the crews of his four ships. Through errors resulting from the limited navigational equipment of the time, La Salle sailed past the Mississippi and landed with his colonists at Matagorda Bay. By the time a temporary fort, called Fort Saint Louis, was built five miles from the mouth of the Lavaca River in the spring of 1685, a series of other misfortunes had reduced the number in the colony to 180 persons.

Yoakum contends that La Salle, determined to find his much sought Mississippi River, set out from the Lavaca River post on April 22, 1686. The historian states that the explorer, along with twenty companions, traveled eastward and estimates that they went as far as the Neches River. Illness and lack of supplies forced the adventurers to return to Fort Saint Louis, but a second expedition was begun on January 12, 1687. It was on this journey that La Salle was killed by one of his men on March 20, 1687.

There are differences of opinion as to the location of La Salle's murder. Four historians give calculations based upon the journal of Henri Joutel, a companion of La Salle; E.W. Cole maintains that the murder was committed near Larrison Creek in present Cherokee County; Francis Parkman places it in the vicinity of the southern branch of the Trinity River; H.H. Bolton, the Brazos River; C.E. Castaneda, along the banks of the Navasota River. Some local residents have even another opinion. They insist the murder occurred in the vicinity of Village Creek in Hardin County. If this is true, it could be the first known murder committed in the Big Thicket.

Two years after the death of La Salle, a Spanish expedition was reported to have traversed the outskirts of the Big Thicket. The government of Spain had previously laid claim to Texas as a result of the conquest of Mexico by Cortez in 1519. Hearing of the activities of the French in Texas, the King of Spain sent Captain Alonzo de Leon with an expedition into the disputed area. On April 22, 1689, De Leon arrived at Fort Saint Louis only to find that it had already been destroyed by a band of savage Indians. In March, 1690, De Leon led a second expedition, composed of soldiers and priests, into East Texas with the purpose of establishing missions. One source contends that the group passed along the northern part of the Big Thicket near the present town of Moscow.

Although Spanish, French, and later Anglo-American activities continued in East Texas for many years following the first expeditions, Spain was generally recognized as the rightful owner of the area by the early 1800's. A treaty was signed in 1819 between Spain and the United States, establishing the Sabine River as the boundary between the two countries.

CHAMP-D' ASILE

During the early 1800's the colony Champ-d' Asile appeared near the present town of Liberty on the Trinity River. The settlement was unique in nature because it was established by a group of Frenchmen without the approval of Spain. The question of why the French chose to settle in the Spanish territory in 1818 may have at least two answers. The most popular version is found in two books, *Le Texas* and *L' Heroine du Texas,* published in France in 1819. Both accounts lead the reader to believe that Champ-d'Asile was settled by a group of French political and military exiles, who, after the defeat of Napoleon, dreamed of finding happiness in farming rather than in fighting. The other belief is based on an anonymous letter written by a young French refugee who lived at Champ-d'Asile. He suggests that the settlement was the result of the colonization scheme of two French officers, Generals Charles and Henri Lallemand, who could not accept the French defeat in Europe and dreamed of establishing a new empire in America. Throughout the letter the author indicates that he was a soldier on a military expedition rather than a farmer engaged in agriculture.

At any rate, the colony was short-lived, lasting only five months. The hardships which they encountered, along with the hostile attitude of the Spanish, caused the bold Frenchmen to abandon the settlement in 1819 and seek refuge on Galveston Island.

Reference was made both in book and in the published anonymous letter about an incident of violence committed near the French settlement which involved two Frenchmen who were eaten by a band of savage Indians. The letter and the book, *Le Texas,* an account based on fact, mention only two members of the colony, Fallot and Albert, as being the unfortunate victims. *L' Heroine du Texas,* a romanticized novel, portrays a more vivid picture. Although the source cannot be taken entirely for the truth, there exists some basis for the story. It appears that while the colonists were in the process of departing the settlement, the two Frenchmen spotted deer on the opposite bank of the Trinity River and decided to try their luck at killing them. When the hunters failed to return after several hours, the colonists became alarmed and formed a party to investigate their whereabouts. The following is an account of their findings:

> Scarcely had we advanced a hundred paces into the forest when we caught sight of about sixty savages sitting in a circle, appearing very preoccupied. See-

ing on the ground the arms and the shredded clothes of our comrades, we suspected what had happened. The officer gave the command to fire, which command was so well executed that about twenty were left lying, the remainder taking flight, most of them wounded, hotly pursued by our men. One of the colonists succeeded in overtaking and dispatching two with his bayonet.

The party then returned to the spot of the horrible feast and noticed the still-quivering limbs of the two unfortunate men. Their remains were taken back to Champ-d'Asile and buried beneath a cypress tree.

EARLY ANGLO-AMERICAN SETTLERS

Several years after the French abandoned Champ'd'Asile, the first permanent settlers began moving into the Big Thicket. There is a joke among some of the present residents of the area that they are somewhat reluctant to trace their family tree very far back for fear they might discover their ancestors came to Texas only one step ahead of the law. In truth, most early settlers in East Texas were respectable farmers obsessed with the pioneer spirit, men who wanted only to improve their way of life. However, the statement concerning questionable characters had basis and originated in the early 1800's when East Texas was particularly attractive to the criminal element. Beginning in 1806 and continuing for fifteen years, Spain and the United States observed what was known as the Neutral Ground policy. The neutral area, over which neither government had jurisdiction, was a strip of land extending between the Sabine and Arroyo Hondo Rivers in the present state of Louisiana. This strip of land naturally became a haven for desperadoes and renegades of all sorts. Travel became so hazardous for traders and others who ventured through the neutral strip that in 1810 and 1812 both governments were compelled to send armed expeditions to expel outlaws. When the United States gained control of the disputed land, a number of the criminals were reported to have drifted into the Big Thicket, taking their criminal tendencies with them.

THOMAS D. YOCUM

The most notorious band of outlaws who operated in the neutral strip was the Yocum gang. Several members of the group had previously been part of the John A. Murrel gang, well-known thieves and highwaymen operating in the lands along the lower Mississippi River. The Yocums settled in the western part of the neutral area around present day Many, Louisiana, but these outlaws often ventured into the regions west of the Sabine and played upon the law abiding population.

One story goes that in 1822 Matthew Yocum, a member of the gang, courted a young lady by the name of Susan Collier who lived east of San Augustine. Fearful of a serious relationship, the father of the girl, Robert Collier, forbade Yocum to return and persuaded Susan to marry Charles Chandler. Yocum, aided by Susan's uncle, James Collier, who was married to a Yocum sister and was also a member of the Yocum gang, murdered James' brother, Robert Collier, and started to San Augustine to kill Chandler. However, Chandler killed both his assailants in the encounter.

Later, other members of the Yocum gang killed a Louisiana man and kidnapped his Negro wife and mulatto children with the intention of selling them as slaves in Texas. Their attempts were thwarted when David Renfro and other neighbors drove the

Yocums out of Louisiana and returned the woman and children to their home.

Early records show that two members of the Yocum gang migrated into the Big Thicket prior to 1830, for in that year Matthew G. White, the alcalde in Liberty, wrote Stephen F. Austin for advice as to how to deal with:

> two certain men who for the basest of crimes — to-wit — the kidnapping of a whole family of colored persons and attempting to sell them after they had murdered the father as is supposed — were driven across the Sabine and their houses burned . . . now these men are attempting to locate themselves in this district... afford us some clue to the method by which we may rid ourselves of such persons as are a great pest and annoyance to our settlement.

One of the two men mentioned in White's letter was Thomas D. Yocum who settled in the Liberty district in the westernmost part of the Big Thicket. While a new environment has often changed the life of a fugitive from one of crime and avarice to one of more peaceful harmony, Thomas Yocum only saw Texas through the eyes of a vulture, seeing for himself more opportunity for prey. He built a country tavern in what is now the small community of Westbury near Pine Island Bayou between Beaumont and Sour Lake. The inn was nestled in a pecan grove near the Old Spanish Trail at that time referred to as the Atascosito Trail. Cattlemen drove their herds over this trail on a west-east course to the markets in New Orleans. Yocum's prey were the cowboys who stopped for lodging along the way. One can envision the grim smile which must have appeared on the old man's face as he heard the sounds of cattle coming in the distance. It is said he would ride out to the road and as the cattlemen approached, he would wave and in his most amiable manner, offer them accommodations for the night. Often in his place, Yocum sent his attractive step-daughter to the road to lure the cowpokes to the premises. At the country inn the guests were treated to fine cooking, an evening of fun and small talk, and a warm bed, all for a small fee. They were invited to stop again on their return trip home from New Orleans. Remembering the pleasant evening spent at the inn, many a cowhand did return — this time with a money belt filled with shining gold coins. Sometimes the men would come back together, but, at other times, a lone traveler, who had stayed to spend more time in the Creole city would appear. It was he who fitted into Yocum's nefarious plan. People became curious after several men, all last seen at the inn, failed to return to their homes. Suspicion arose even more when a number of fine American horses generally ridden by travelers were seen grazing near the Yocum place. These larger horses were in strong contrast to the small Spanish ponies used by most of the natives.

A letter written in December, 1836, when the Republic of Texas was less than a year old, shows how the infamous reputation of Yocum had spread. At this time the hungry troops of the Texas army relied on the scattered cattle herds of Southeast Texas for their food and their horses. William S. Fisher, acting secretary of war, instructed Colonel Logan at Liberty "to use every exertion within your power to supply the post at Galveston island with beef . . . . You will find at Pine Island, men by the name of D. Yokum (and others) . . . who form a party . . . and considered rather dangerous. Be on your guard while among them. I don't wish you to have any collision with these people."

Settlers began to avoid the Yocum inn as they would the devil. Children of the settlement were forbidden to go near the mysterious dwelling and Negro slaves would tremble at the mention of the name Yocum. A story is told of a Negro girl named Lou Turner who lived on a nearby plantation. Lou was an unruly individual and was often disciplined for her actions. After one such encounter with her master, Lou, pouting over her treatment, ran deep into the woods far from the plantation house. There she ran upon Yocum and his trusted slave hiding some of his stolen gold in a small brick vault. Yocum wanted to kill Lou on the spot but his slave interceded, and after Lou promised she would never reveal the secret of the hidden gold, Yocum let her return unharmed to her master.

Then there was the organ grinder who was not as lucky as the slave girl. He and his monkey appeared at the village one day riding a dappled gray horse. Children of the settlement quickly gathered around the odd pair and stared in disbelief for they had never seen a monkey clothed in a dainty green velvet suit and wearing a red satin cap. As the quaint-looking man began to turn the crank on his brightly colored hand organ, the monkey automatically started a comical jig. The whimsical little monk delighted the children for hours as he danced merrily to the repetitious sound of the music box. By night, the organ grinder's box was heavy with coins dropped in by children and adults alike. People knew the performers had gone to the inn that night but did not become suspicious until days later when they noticed the gray horse grazing alone in the fields beyond the pecan grove. The broken and battered organ and the monkey's bloodstained little green suit lay hidden in the grass.

Another story is told about an unsuspecting man who appeared at the inn one evening asking for directions about the trail which crossed Pine Island Bayou. He was well-dressed and wore a gold chain and watch and rode a fine bay horse. Yocum cordially agreed to show the man the way. After rid-

53

PINE ISLAND BAYOU

THIS GROVE OF pecan trees near Pine Island Bayou once surrounded the infamous Yocum Inn where many an early cowpoke disappeared mysteriously.

ing out to the trail, Yocum reportedly killed the man and returned with his valuables. Upon his return, Mrs. Yocum inquired as to how much cash the man carried. Her husband answered that the stranger had only six bits in coin. Mrs. Yocum then remarked that a man who put on a front like that with fine clothes, a good horse and a gold watch and chain, got what he deserved and should have been killed. A guest in an adjoining room overheard the conversation. He promptly slipped out the door, saddled his horse and swiftly rode away.

Finally, in October, 1841, several citizens, determined to restore law and order, banded together and went to the inn but found that Yocum had escaped. Among other evidence, a Negro showed them the bones of one traveler in a well and those on the nearby prairie. Convinced of Yocum's guilt, the citizens ordered his family to leave the country and burned the inn.

Next, they set out after Yocum and succeeded in capturing him on Spring Creek in Montgomery County. They gave him a brief time to repent for a lifetime of crime, then they shot him.

Thomas Yocum had a son, Christopher, who returned to Southeast Texas approximately a year later to be with his wife. The Jefferson County sheriff, fearing for Christopher's life, arrested him and locked him in the jail at Beaumont for safekeeping. This precaution failed, for the morning after the day of his incarceration, Christopher was found hanged and with a ten-penny nail driven into the top of his head. Unhappily, Christopher was known to have been the best one of the Yocums.

Clues in the lynchings of both Thomas D. Yocum and his son, Christopher, pointed to the actions of the "Regulators," citizens of East Texas who, unsanctioned by the law, attempted to bring an end to what they deemed unlawfulness. In January, 1842, Sam Houston, president of the Republic, issued a "Proclamation Against the Regulators" noting that "certain individuals, residents of the counties of Liberty and Jefferson . . . have murdered one Thomas D. Yocum . . . burnt his late residence . . . and driven his widow and children from their home." He then instructed all district attorneys of the several judicial districts to prosecute the law violators.

Many people have searched fruitlessly for the brick vault where the slave girl, Lou, is rumored to have seen Yocum and his servant hiding his ill-gotten money. Throughout Texas there are many stories of unfound buried gold and perhaps Yocum's gold like these legendary stories will lie forever buried among the huge trees which once surrounded the mysterious inn.

THE HARDIN FAMILY

During the same era, fugitives migrated to Texas from lands farther to the East. One of the most interesting examples involved members of the well-known Hardin family after whom Hardin County was named. The Hardin brothers, Augustine Blackburn, Benjamin Watson, William, Franklin, and Milton A., along with their parents, Swan and Jerusha Hardin, migrated from Maury County, Tennessee and settled along the Trinity River in present Liberty County in the 1820's. At this time Texas was a Mexican territory since Mexico had won its independence from Spain in 1821.

The Hardin family had been accused of crimes before leaving Tennessee. Swan Hardin and his sons, excluding the youngest son, Milton, were under indictment in Maury County for the murders of Isaac Porter and William H. Williamson. The killings resulted from a feud between the Hardin and Porter families. The circumstances which led to the feud are undetermined but it is said that the Hardins shot and killed Porter and Williamson in self-defense. Since several members of the Porter family were important officeholders in Maury County, Tennessee, the Hardins felt that a fair trial was unlikely, and, as a result, Augustine and Franklin fled before being arrested. Swan Hardin and sons, Benjamin W. and William, were arrested and pled not guilty to the murder charge. Swan received a separate trial in Rutherford County in March, 1826, and was found not guilty of murder but guilty of being an accessory to manslaughter. His punishment was imprisonment for three months and being "branded on the brawn of the left thumb." Benjamin and William escaped before their case was tried.

By 1827 all five Hardin brothers and their parents had left Tennessee and were living in the Liberty district. United States authorities made efforts to extradite the brothers as indicated in a letter written by an official of the United States to the government of Mexico in 1828:

> I have instructions from my Government to demand the delivery of four persons that are found accused of having committed one of the most atrocious murders in the State of Tennessee, and who have fled and taken refuge in the State of Texas and Coahuila. These persons fled from justice after a law against them was published in legal form by a Grande Jury the 21st of October of 1825 . . . .
>
> My government knows very well that it has not the right to force the delivery of these men; but delivering assassins and forgers on the request of a friendly power is an act of civility between civilized nations. Situated respectively as the countries are with relation to each other, the blackest crimes can be committed in our territories with impunity if the criminal, in order to free himself from punishment,

has only to pass the boundary. In one of the articles of the Treaty of Friendship, Navigation and Trade, it agrees in reciprocal delivery of fugitives that have committed the crime of murder; . . . .

The government of Mexico, in turn, notified officers in Nacogdoches to apprehend the fugitives, to deliver them to Nacogdoches, and to take all precautions to prevent their escape until they could be turned over to the United States government.

In August, 1828, Stephen F. Austin received a message from the Mexican officials that William and Franklin had been arrested. The officers instructed Austin to arrest Benjamin and Augustine Hardin. Austin promptly formed an eight man militia and marched from San Felipe to the Liberty district but failed to capture the two Hardins. It was believed that the brothers had been warned beforehand by friends and had fled their homes. Austin then assigned his duty of apprehending the Hardins to George Orr, an official in the Liberty area. Orr later turned the assignment over to Captain Hugh B. Johnston. Since both Orr and Johnston were neighbors of the Hardins, and were no doubt in sympathy with them, their attempts to arrest Benjamin and Augustine were probably intentionally futile. At any rate, the pair was never apprehended. Although William and Franklin had been arrested previously by the Mexican government, there is no known evidence that they were ever turned over to the United States government. The United States took no further actions against the Hardins after 1829.

In the years that followed, members of the Hardin family were rated among the leading citizens of Southeast Texas. Augustine B. Hardin, in particular, took an active part in the Texas bid for independence. He represented the town of Liberty in the Consultation of 1835 and again at the Convention of 1836 at Washington-on-the-Brazos, where he was one of the signers of the Declaration of Independence.

MIGRATION INTO TEXAS

After she won her independence and established a republic, Texas experienced a notable increase in the Anglo-American population. It was apparent that the westward movement was in full bloom by the statistics of 1847 which reported approximately 135,000 persons residing in the state of Texas, an increase over an estimated 20,000 in 1831. Those who settled in Southeast Texas came chiefly from the states of Louisiana, Mississippi, and Alabama. Less numerous were persons from Tennessee, Missouri, Arkansas, Kentucky, and Illinois.

THE ALABAMAS AND THE COUSHATTAS

As the early settlers moved into the area of the Big Thicket, they encountered two related tribes of Indians, the Alabamas and the Coushattas. The Indians themselves had migrated from the Southeastern states only a short time earlier. The Coushattas were known to have crossed the Sabine River in 1807 and to have settled along the Trinity approximately three leagues below the village of Salcedo. It is not certain when the Alabamas entered Texas, but it is said to have been in the same period. They first settled near the Sabine and later on the west bank of the Neches River.

From the first contacts with the Anglo-Americans up to the present day, both tribes of Indians were found to be very friendly and hospitable. In fact, the peaceful nature of the Indians was sometimes severely tried by unprincipled members of the white race who plundered their crops and stock for no better reason than that they were Indians.

One example of hostile attitudes shown the East Texas Indians by the Whites is found in the account of a white man who stole his Indian neighbor's hogs. The story goes that the Alabama Indian had several hogs pinned up behind his small shack. One morning when he went out to feed the animals, he discovered that they were gone. The Alabama suspected a particular white man who lived nearby, but hesitated to immediately accuse him of the theft. Soon after, the Indian noticed a large amount of smoke coming from his neighbor's smokehouse. His patience lasted long enough for the meat to cook and the neighbor to leave, then the Alabama walked over to the smokehouse, jacked up one corner of the building, crawled under, and hauled away all of his smoked hogs, now in the form of bacon and hams. Of course, the white man was enraged by the Indian's defiant act and filed charges against him which resulted in the Indian's arrest. What the white man did not anticipate was that the judge who heard the facts of the case was tired of seeing the Indians abused and ruled that the hogs belonged to the Indian — so the bacon and hams were his, too.

On one occasion in 1836, some citizens of Liberty County charged a group of Coushatta Indians with horse stealing. In spite of the fact that the Indians denied the crime and that little evidence was found against them, five Coushattas were murdered. The Indians presented their grievance to Maribeau B. Lamar, president of the Texas Republic. An investigation supported the Indians' plea of innocence, but seemingly nothing was done to punish the Liberty County residents. As a result of the trouble, a number of the Coushattas moved into northeast Texas and settled along the Red River.

Another act of violence allegedly took place among the Alabama Indians in the year 1847. It did not occur as the result of any depredation by the whites, but because of fear existing in the Indian tribe itself. According to the late Dr. W.W. Anderson of Kountze, the following story was told to him by his grandfather, James Barclay, who was appointed by General Sam Houston in 1837 as the first Indian agent for the Alabamas.

A strange epidemic which killed the young as well as the old had swept through one of the small East Texas Indian villages. Desperate to find the cause of the unknown malady, some of the more superstitious readily placed the blame on a particular old woman who was rumored to be practicing the age-old art of witchcraft. Not all agreed with the accusation, however, and it seemed that intrabribal war might take place at any time. One night as the old woman sat in her hut before her small fire, two young Alabama braves stole in quietly and decapitated her. As the ugly wrinkled head rolled onto the floor, the braves took sticks lighted from her fire and turned her hut into a mass of flames.

When the news of the slaying spread, the faction who had been in favor of keeping the accused witch alive was holding a meeting at Agent Barclay's house. They were already dressed in their war paint, but Agent Barclay persuaded them to let the government mete out punishment to the culprits.

The State of Texas moved the Alabama and Coushatta Indians onto a reservation in the Big Thicket in the 1850's. The reservation was at first encircled with a high fence. It is not known just why the fence was built, whether it was to keep the Indians in or the Whites out. But before long, sections of the fence began to disappear, carried off little by little by the surrounding white neighbors.

CATTLE RUSTLING

As adventuresome emigrants continued moving into the Thicket from the "older states," communities came into existence and roads appeared. Prior to the Civil War, settlements were few and roads were little more than mere trails. One of the most traveled routes through the Big Thicket was the Opelousas Trail, a branch of the Atascosito Trail, that led from Texas to Louisiana over which ranchers drove their cattle to market. It was particularly along this route that cattle rustling flourished.

ACCORDING TO LEGEND, the killing of the old Alabama Indian woman in the Big Thicket was probably the last execution for witchcraft to occur in the United States.

(Drawing appeared in the *Beaumont Enterprise*, April 2, 1959).

The road crossed Batson's Prairie where great herds of cattle grazed. These herds were raided so often by cattle thieves that the early citizens of the area banded into a vigilante group called "the night riders."

One story is often told about a cattle thief by the name of Vailma Raibee who was caught by the group one night in the process of slaughtering a steer. The night riders decided to use Raibee as an example to deter any further stealing of cattle. With hands and feet tied, Raibee was placed into the hide of the freshly-killed animal. The hide was then sewed around him leaving only his head and feet sticking out. It was an old Indian form of torture. As the hide dried, it contracted and slowly choked the victim to death. During the process, the victim suffered further torture from ants and other carnivorous insects attracted by the raw hide.

The incident may have deterred cattle rustling for some time on Batson's Prairie, but by the 1880's the theft of cattle and hogs was the most prevalent crime in Hardin County and was to continue well into the twentieth century and exists even today.

One example of cattle rustling in the later period took place in the summer of 1907 along the western edge of the Thicket. A Beaumont newspaper described it as: "The most gigantic efforts at wholesale cattle stealing ever attempted in this section of Texas at any stage of early life on the frontier, if not in all Texas, . . ."

The account stated that a party of several men made a request at the Texas and New Orleans railroad terminal in the town of Nome for four freight cars to be loaded with cattle which they desired to ship. The cars arrived, and the men started corralling the cattle for shipment. Several people of the area noticed that each morning there was an additional number of cattle confined in the pens. Not knowing who was assembling the large shipment and wanting to find a good market for their cattle, also, some big stockmen became interested. Finally, George Caswell, a stockman from Sour Lake, decided to investigate. He rode to one of the pens where the cattle were corralled and approached one of the strangers. During the conversation, he noticed that the cattle were branded with brands of many stock farmers and that among the lot were two of his own. The shocked stockman promptly left and reported his discovery to several of his friends. A posse was immediately formed, but when the citizens arrived at the pens, the cattle had been turned out, and the man who had been tending them was gone. Obviously, Caswell had aroused the suspicion of the stranger. Further investigation into the matter indicated that the thieves were composed of a number of Hardin, Jefferson, and Liberty County toughs who had previously been implicated in several oil field rows in the Batson, Saratoga, and Sour Lake fields. Having heard tales of cattle rustling in the old days and believing other cattle robberies might occur, the posse of cattlemen were eager to apprehend and punish the culprits. They conducted an extensive search in the vicinity of the Big Thicket for days, but were never successful in apprehending the thieves.

FORMATION OF HARDIN COUNTY

Early residents of the Big Thicket were often accustomed to handling their own problems. In 1858, the year that Hardin County was formed, the State, attempting to organize the county government, sent Judge White, a magistrate from Jefferson County, to prepare for elections and to set up the courts. The judge appointed a jury commission to draw up a jury and gave each member a book in which to record the cases due for trial when he returned to hold court. Judge White was quite surprised when he returned and found that all matters had been settled.

Those left in charge had hanged eight men and shot three. Several days earlier, four other men, deemed lawless, had been hanged at the little town of Concord on Pine Island Bayou.

BOOTH-GUEDRY FEUD

It was in the period before the Civil War that a feud started between two pioneering East Texas families, the Booths and the Guedrys. The feud lasted for many years, resulted in several shootings, and covered an area of Texas much larger than the Big Thicket area. The story is well-known, for it has been told by several historians, including the famous Texas folklorist, J. Frank Dobie. There are discrepancies in the story, but most local historians who have checked the records agree with the following account.

The Robert E. Booth family and the Ursin Guedry family moved into East Texas in the 1830's and 1840's respectively and settled near the Sabine River approximately nine miles north of the town of Orange. During these early years in Texas, Robert E. Booth was a farmer and Ursin Guedry operated a ferry which crossed the Sabine. Both families were not only neighbors but were obviously good friends, because when Robert Booth died in 1848, Guedry signed on a $20,000 bond as sureties for Booth's widow, Elizabeth, as administratrix of the estate. On August 23, 1848, Guedry was also appointed by the Court along with two other men to appraise Booth's property. It is not certain when the trouble between the two families first began, but it may have started over problems in the administration of Booth's estate, because on July 3, 1851, Guedry petitioned the Court to be released from the sureties bond.

However, another event caused animosities to surface. Back in the early days it was the responsibility of communities in Texas to help build roads.

When a man came of age, he was expected to either pay a tax or work on the road. On August, 1851, a road which went past the Geudry and Booth properties was being constructed from the Sabine River to the Tevis ferry on the Neches River near Beaumont. Ursin Guedry was appointed overseer of the road building crew near his home, and two sons of the deceased Booth, Rueben and Robert, worked as laborers on the road. Difficulties arose between the two brothers and another crew member which caused Rueben and Robert to want to quit their job. As a result, Guedry and the brothers argued, tempers flared, and Rueben and Robert were shot and killed by Guedry. The killings may have been acts of self-defense, because there is no record of Guedry's indictment. Now there was another Booth brother, seventeen-year-old John, who witnessed the deaths of his brothers and vowed to Guedry that he would one day avenge their deaths by killing him.

John's mother remarried in November of 1851, and soon after, John moved three hundred miles west settling near the Nueces River in South Texas. Guedry later moved from Orange County to Hardin County three miles east of Sour Lake on Little Pine Island Bayou. The years passed and Ursin Guedry probably forgot the threats of vengeance. But John Booth did not, because in 1861 he began to boast again about what he was going to do to Guedry. Three hundred miles was a far distance in those days, but it did not take long before the news reached Guedry in Hardin County. John was still in no hurry though and let Guedry worry and fret.

The following fall John mapped out a route from where he lived on the Nueces River to Hardin County. He had friends stationed with fresh horses every thirty to forty miles along the way, his own pony express. John then went to visit a neighbor and asked if he would verify that he was there at his house on that day, at that hour, and record it in the family Bible. The neighbor readily agreed, and before witnesses, the date was written as the twentieth of October, seven o'clock, 1861. John Booth cordially but promptly said good-night and rode away on his mission. Two days later a stranger appeared in the Big Thicket asking for directions to the Guedry farm. That evening Guedry was dead. On the twenty-fifth John returned to his neighbor's house and again requested that the day and hour be recorded in the family Bible. Soon Booth was arrested by Texas Rangers for the murder of Guedry. When the case was tried the recordings in the Bible were strong evidence for the defense. The jury, unconvinced that a man could travel a distance of three hundred miles and back in four days and five nights, set John Booth free. Booth began to talk proudly about his exciting caper, knowing that if a man is found innocent on a charge, he cannot be retried. He later joined the Army of the Confederacy.

Revenge was sweet for John Booth for many years, but, as often happens, one must eventually pay for one's crimes. It is said that John had only one child, a son named Robert, who was shot and killed by Guedry's two sons. He later lost his fortune and died, a broken man, in the Home for Confederate Soldiers in Austin.

MAJOR JOE N. DARK

Another widely discussed crime of the Big Thicket occurred in 1861, the year Ursin Guedry was killed and the year the Civil War began. It revolved around a prominent early settler, Major Joe N. Dark, who lived on Batson's Prairie. Major Dark was a man of many vocations, working at one time or another as a soldier, rancher, farmer, civil engineer, county surveyor, and doctor.

When the South seceded from the Union, Major Dark and a good friend of his, Captain A.B. Mitchell, decided to enter the Confederate Army. Before

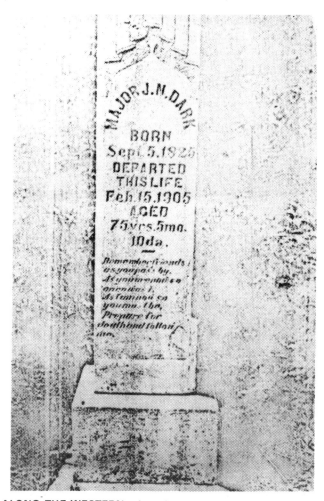

ALONG THE WESTERN edge of the Big Thicket near the community of Moss Hill, lies the remote grave of Major J.N. Dark. The epitaph inscribed on the tombstone is unusual:

"Remember friends
As you pass by,
As you are now so
Once was I,
As I am now so
You must be,
Prepare for
Death and follow me."

leaving his home, the Major sold his large herd of cattle for a considerable sum of money. It was rumored that the money was hidden somewhere in his house.

Living nearby in the Pine Ridge community was the Magnes family, consisting of the mother and two sons, Tom and John. The other settlers knew little of them except that Mrs. Magnes professed to be a doctor, claiming cures for cancer and other dread diseases. Her son, Tom, was reported to have belonged to a notorious band of Mississippi River pirates. The family built a two-story log house and several small cabins for the patients who came from great distances for the magical cures. Some of these patients entered the primitive clinic and were never seen again. It was believed that they had been robbed and murdered and then buried in the dense Thicket which surrounded the dwellings.

At any rate, Tom Magnes apparently heard rumors about Major Dark's hidden money. On the night of September 16, 1861, he, with two others, G.H. Willis and Austin Chessher, attempted to rob and murder the Major and his family. About midnight, the men rode to the home of Major Dark and called out to him. Knowing Willis and thinking the visit was a friendly one, Dark invited the men to wait on his porch while he dressed. As soon as the Major opened the door, Willis shot at him, missing his target. Alarmed by the noise, Mrs. Dark began to stir in her room and was immediately wounded by Chessher. Meanwhile, Dark was able to find his gun and fire at Chessher, killing him instantly. Willis and Magnes fled, escaping into the nearby Thicket. The local citizens were especially angry that a man who was at the point of going away to serve the Confederacy had been attacked.

Close to the Magnes home was a typical "bay gall," or low place which collected water and where the sweet bay, red bay, and the gall berries usually grew. Accounts vary, but one source states that it was in the Magnes bay gall that Tom Magnes was believed to be hiding. The posse took John Magnes to the bay gall and forced him to call his brother. Thinking the way was clear, Tom came out of hiding and was quickly apprehended. Soon after, Willis was found in Tyler County. Both were taken to the courthouse at Old Hardin, the county seat of Hardin County at that time, where the citizens gathered to decide the fate of the fugitives. While Willis was writing his confession in a room on the second floor, a commotion arose outside around Tom Magnes. Addressing the crowd, Dark's friend, Captain Mitchell, drew a line on the ground and asked those who wanted the culprits hanged to cross the line. All stepped over. Learning of their decision, Willis fainted and never signed the confession. Subsequently, Magnes and Willis were hanged from two huge trees at the edge of town. When Mrs. Magnes heard of her son's death, she was reported to have said that Tom got what he deserved and calmly asked for the hanging rope to tie her cow.

Two relics from the Dark and Magnes families survive the past and are in the possession of the Mayo family whose ancestors were early Thicket pioneers. One is a violin that belonged to Tom Magnes; the other, the door from Major Dark's house into which bullets were fired during the assault.

KAISER'S BURNOUT

During the Civil War, no major battles took place on Big Thicket soil, but stories circulated frequently of war-related activities. The best known of these is one about the time a Confederate officer, Captain Jim Kaiser*, set fire to a portion of the Thicket in the northwestern part of Hardin County. The purpose of the fire was to drive out a group of East

_____

* Also spelled Kyser or Keyser.

Texas men who were avoiding going to war. Some have called them conscientious objectors, saying that they did not believe in slavery; others have contended that they were simply deserters. Whatever their reasons, they found the Big Thicket an ideal place to hide.

For almost four years, the Jayhawkers, as they came to be called, hid out in the dense woods. A Confederate officer, Captain Charles Bullock, who, with his company of men, was stationed at Woodville. This calvary made several attempts to capture the band of fugitives but were always unsuccessful. The Thicket was the Jayhawkers' home, and they could easily elude their pursuers.

The hunted men lived off the land, for wild game was abundant, but they obviously felt that life could be more pleasant if they had other supplies. They established a system of underground communication with some of their sympathetic neighbors whereby they would collect honey from the bee trees, which were numerous in that area of the Thicket, and leave it at a designated spot. In return the Jayhawkers would get the staples they needed such as flour, corn meal, coffee, and tobacco. The small community called Honey Island got its name from the fact that it was the place where the honey was deposited.

By 1864 the South was desperate. She needed men, money, and supplies. It was then that Captain Jim Kaiser from Polk County appeared, determined to provide some of the men from the ranks of the Jayhawkers. He waited until the opportune time when the woods were dry and the wind was right, then set fire to the forest, forming a flaming horseshoe around the spot where the recalcitrants were alleged to be hiding. Next, he and his men quickly rode to the opening that they had left in the woods and waited for the Jayhawkers to come out. They waited, but no one came. Finally, Kaiser and his soldiers gave up and returned to their head-

ONE OF THE MOST popular stories depicting Big Thicket law-lessness is the Kaiser Burnout of Civil War days. In the 1940's a talented young writer, Larry Jean Fisher, wrote a play about the interesting incident which involved Confederate forces attempting to "burn-out" a group of deserters. The first actors (above) were Saratoga High School students, descendants of the original Jayhawkers. (Courtesy Lamar Library - Fisher Collection.)

quarters. Many think that the evaders were warned earlier and were gone before the fires were set. Whatever happened, the incident was a source of embarrassment to Captain Kaiser and his troops for many years.

The fire burned for two days, destroying 2,000 acres of woodlands and killing numerous birds and animals. It remained an area of scorched earth until around 1930 when a lumber company planted it with pine trees. Lush and green again today, the site of the burnout is visible only to the trained observer.

The burning of the woods was the last determined effort made by the Confederates to bring the Jayhawkers into the army. The Civil War soon ended and the fugitives drifted back to their farms and families. Some of the men carried the stigma of being "Jayhawkers" to their graves, but most redeemed themselves by convincing their neighbors that they, too, were honorable and dutiful citizens and that the actions they had taken were in the name of what they thought to be right.

Kaiser's Burnout, as it came to be called, became such a popular story in East Texas that it attracted the attention of a talented young man named Larry Jean Fisher. Fisher, then living in Beaumont, moved to Saratoga where he became better acquainted with the Big Thicket, its people and its history. In the early 1940's he wrote a play based on the story of the Kaiser Burnout. The play was first presented in Saratoga with a cast of Saratoga high school students, descendants of the original Jayhawkers; and later the play was given in several other cities in Texas and Louisiana.

Draft dodgers from World Wars I and II reportedly also hid out successfully in the deep woods. Those who are around today are said to be still true to their convictions, whatever they might be.

PERIOD OF RECONSTRUCTION

While the Civil War temporarily halted the westward movement, the years that followed showed many planters looking to the West again. The population of Texas increased some 94.5 per cent between the years 1870 and 1880. More specifically, the counties which comprised the Big Thicket evidenced a similar population growth. Statistics indicate that the 1870 to 1890 period showed increases of from approximately 1,460 to 3,956 persons in Hardin County, from 4,414 to 4,999 persons in Liberty County, from 8,707 to 10,332 persons in Polk County and from 5,010 to 10,877 persons in Tyler County.

The few records which have been preserved and other material which is available relating to the Big Thicket during this period indicate that besides the increase in population, progress was being shown in other ways. Sawmills and railroads appeared throughout the area and led to the beginning of many new communities. Civilization for the first time started closing in on the forest.

Although the post-Civil War period was one of growth and renewed activities, the years immediately following the war were at first very trying ones. As was the case in the rest of the South, the citizens of Southeast Texas experienced some difficulties associated with Reconstruction.

One historical reference to this period is found in an unpublished account of the Big Thicket written by Frances Pitts Norvell. Allegedly told by the first district judge of the area, Henry B. Pedigo, the story illustrates how some citizens dealt with one of the problems. A Negro carpetbagger, living north of Tyler County, had stolen a horse and buggy from a poor widow whose husband had been killed in the Civil War. Learning of the theft and hearing news that the Negro was slowly traveling south, some of the men of the community decided to mete out justice. Knowing also that the carpetbagger would pass through the community of Chester in Tyler County, they traveled there quickly and awaited his appearance. When the victim arrived, the men killed him and buried him in the nearby woods. What the men did not realize was that another Negro had watched their activities and reported them to the military officials in Woodville. The next day the officers went to Chester, arrested the men, and returned with them to Woodville. Further investigation into the matter took the officials to the spot where the body was reported to have been buried. When the men dug into the grave, instead of the body of the carpetbagger, they found a big black hog! After several attempts to locate the dead Negro, the case was abandoned.

According to the story, what actually happened was that when the arrested men were in Woodville, the women of Chester killed the black hog, dug up

the body of the victim, and replaced it with that of the animal. The perplexed Negro who had reported the killing left Chester rather hurriedly and was never seen again.

Another story of violence occurring in the Big Thicket during the Reconstruction era is found in the autobiography of the infamous John Wesley Hardin, a relative of Augustine B. Hardin, mentioned before as a prominent early settler of the Big Thicket. John Wesley Hardin, son of an itinerant Methodist preacher, was born on May 26, 1853, in Bonham, Texas, growing up during the Civil War and the Reconstruction period.

The following quotation appears in his autobiography and seems to sum up his feelings as a young boy regarding the troubled times of Reconstruction:

> Principles of the Southern cause loomed in my mind. I had seen Abe Lincoln burned and shot in effigy so often that I looked upon him as a very demon incarnate, who was waging a relentless and cruel war on the South to rob her of her most sacred rights.

By 1865 young Hardin and his family had moved and settled in the town of Sumpter in Trinity County, north of the Big Thicket. Living there, the boy often visited an uncle, William Barnett Hardin, who owned a plantation about four miles north of Livingston in Polk County.

John Wesley was to visit the uncle for the last time in the fall of 1868. In his autobiography, he related that he and a cousin, Barnett Jones, had a wrestling bout with a Negro named Mage. Hardin failed to comment on the fairness of the match; nonetheless, it ended with Mage the loser. The Negro became angry, vowed to kill Hardin, and, as

JOHN WESLEY HARDIN, the famous outlaw who killed his first man near Moscow, Texas, in the northern part of the Big Thicket.

(Picture appeared in the *Houston Post*, December 9, 1946.)

a result, was ordered off the plantation by Uncle Barnett.

Hardin explains that the next morning he left the home of his uncle to return to Sumpter. Soon after he departed, he encountered Mage who was walking along the road carrying a large stick. According to the account, the Negro called Hardin a coward and again vowed to kill him, coming at him with the stick. He hit Hardin, and, as he did, the boy pulled out his pistol and threatened to shoot. Mage did not take the warning, and came at Hardin again. Hardin fired several shots, fatally wounding the Negro.

Hardin states in his book that after the Negro died, he went directly to his father and confessed what he had done. Believing that young Hardin would not receive a fair trial from the Union military forces and the State Police of Reconstruction, his father persuaded him to go into hiding. Thus at the age of fifteen, John Wesley Hardin became a fugitive from the law.

John Wesley never stopped running. A criminal career begun in the Big Thicket lay ahead of him. By the time he was twenty, he was supposed to have killed at least two dozen men, excluding Mexicans and Negroes. He gained for himself the reputation of being the most cold-blooded and deadly killer the Southwest ever produced. He worked full time at hating all Yankees and blamed the feelings which prevailed after the Civil War for his violent career. His notorious life continued until 1895 when he himself was shot by the gunman John Selman in an El Paso saloon.

CHAPTER III

Boom Town

lawlessness

During the first few years of the twentieth century, the Big Thicket communities of Batson, Saratoga, and Sour Lake were quickly transformed from small, peaceful settlements into typical boom towns where lawlessness and vice became the accepted way of life. The discovery of oil in Southeast Texas brought about these changes.

Long before the boom days some individuals believed that petroleum oil existed in the area. As early as 1860 prospecting for the oil began in the Sour Lake district, but the turbulence of the Civil War and the period of stagnation which followed caused all activities to cease.

It was not until 1895 that renewed efforts in the area were successful. The Savage brothers from West Virginia secured leases and developed three wells at Sour Lake which produced approximately fifty barrels of oil a day. The brothers built a small refinery but after various difficulties, they abandoned the field.

Although other efforts were made to locate East Texas oil strata, it was not until the Lucas gusher at Spindletop near Beaumont that notable success was achieved in oil operations. The well came in as a full-fledged gusher on the 10th of January, 1901, spewing oil 225 feet into the air. No one had anticipated such a well, and as a result, no arrangements had been made to stop its flow. It ran wild for nine days before it could be shut off.

News of the oil phenomenon spread almost instantaneously, and before the well was under control, men were there from all directions and from every walk of life. Overnight Beaumont became a bustling town, totally inadequate to accommodate the thousands who came. The newcomers slept anywhere that opportunity offered, on the floor, on the ground, some traveled each night as far away as Houston. The excitement around Spindletop was even greater than that of the California gold rush because advances which had been made in transportation facilities made the oil field more accessible.

From January 10, 1901, to May 10, 1902, 379 wells were drilled at Spindletop. Fully one million barrels of oil were wasted because men would put every dollar they had into an oil well, and when it came in, there would be no available storage tanks for the oil. By 1903 Spindletop had decreased its production considerably.

As Spindletop dwindled, other Southeast Texas oil fields took its place. Two years after the Lucas gusher, almost to the day, a gusher blew in at Sour Lake, and in the same year, oil was discovered in nearby Saratoga and at Batson's Prairie. The oil discoveries brought not only the boomers, but also gamblers, merchants, and women of "light repute," all eager to relieve the oil field worker of his money.

At the time of the boom, Sour Lake was a community of fifteen old shacks, a remnant of another era. In 1845 the town, which derived its name from some twenty-seven mineral springs, was a popular health spa frequented by many wealthy and prominent people. Among the visiting affluent was Sam Houston, who spent a month at the resort in the early 1860's, hoping for some relief from his old war injuries. The Civil War ended this phase of the town's history but the discovery of oil brought another boom.

While the people who came to Sour Lake during the early days of the boom were a different breed from the cultured elite of the 1800's, they brought an excitement to the town which has never before or since been equalled. By the latter part of 1903, Sour Lake had grown into a thriving tent city noted for its fifty-six saloons and one church.

Charlie Jeffries, a worker in the Sour Lake field, recalled years later that about any type saloon could be found in Sour Lake:

> . . . all sizes and quality. House of Lords, a place where the big boys gathered and played pool and rowied around. Derrick Saloon, Big Thicket Saloon, Dad's Saloon (this was a noted hangout for blacklegs and cut-throats). Considering the character of the town, it is almost a waste of words to say that the saloons were well patronized; . . .
>
> As for other evidences of heavy drinking there were plenty of these too, such as empty flasks by the wayside. It was a sight, the number and variety of whiskey bottles lying in the weeds along the paths through the oil field.

The *Beaumont Enterprise* at the time of the boom modestly reported:

> There is also a little of everything that is spicy or sporty to be found in this quarter for the money. At present in appearance it reminds one somewhat of a county fair back east but has rather more of a Buffalo Bill day air about it, for you can find anything from a circus lemonade to a poker game . . . .

When Billy Bryant as a youth of seventeen arrived in Sour Lake in 1903, he found a city of ten thousand people. He recalled one of the "sporty" attractions of the town:

. . . we had lots of fighting among the women . . . I believe Nella Dale and Grace Ashley put on the best bout I ever seen. I think they fought an hour and fifteen minutes before they were separated. And when they quit fighting, they didn't have on enough clothes to wipe out a twenty-two . . . .

Women and men. You could, if you wanted to see a fist fight, if there wasn't one on in the block you was on, walk over to the next block, you'd see it; . . . and the bunch I worked with —I hate to say it — but they was double-tough.

Bryant first worked as an oil-well driller but, because of the many fights, shootings, and general disregard for law and order in Sour Lake during those days, he later became a Hardin County deputy sheriff, a position he held for sixty years. He was a soft-spoken man who was not known to bully lawbreakers, that is, unless they got rough first. The respect that he gained as a lawman is evidenced by his unique but effective way of handling the lawless population. When he heard of trouble such as a fight or a shooting, he often sent word to the offender to come to his place promptly or he would come and get him. His threat was almost always successful. One day a man was killed in a fight in a saloon. When Bryant went to investigate the crime, the killer had left, so the deputy told the people present to send word to him to be at his house the next morning at sunup. Around three the following morning, the man tapped on Bryant's bedroom window, ready to confess his guilt. The lawman told the suspect to go away, that he would not get up at three in the morning to arrest anyone but warned him to be at the jail when he got there. Bryant arrived at seven a.m. and the man was leaning against the jail door.

In addition to the usual rowdiness which accompanied the oil boom in Sour Lake, race problems occurred periodically. Newspaper accounts of the day give evidence that the troubles were always started by the rough element of the town and never sanctioned by the more substantial citizens. However, their disapproval was more from an economic standpoint than from feelings of compassion.

The first indication of any racial trouble began in the early part of February, 1903, when a note circulated around town warning the Negroes to leave Sour Lake immediately or they would be literally driven out or killed outright. Twenty-five black employees left en masse. No one seemed to know the reason for the threat.

The worst racial difficulty, however, occurred the following July. On July 9th, an unprincipled mob of five hundred men, armed with guns and clubs and bent on driving out the Negro workers, gathered before one of the many Sour Lake saloons. Shooting and yelling, the men proceeded on their mission, scouting the town for their victims. Whenever a victim was found, he was marched out and commanded to "run the gauntlet," receiving many a blow along the way. The biggest "find" for the evening was in the Southern Pacific railroad yard. There the rioters encountered 175 Mexicans and Negroes, all employees of the railroad, lodged in several railroad cars. ". . . the trembling, cowering wretches carrying their shoes in their hands were compelled to come out, run the gauntlet and make tracks for Nome." One Mexican who refused to run was so badly beaten over the head, apparently with the butt end of a revolver, that his head was crushed and he was left to die.

The crowd made several more attacks, all without interference, then proceeded into the oil field. Their intentions were to rout out another large group of Negroes who were employed by the Moore-Skinner Company, builders of earthen tanks. For the first time during the night, they met resistance. Colonel Ed Ketchem, an old soldier and a former chief of police who was in charge of the Negroes, announced that he had no intention of letting his men be mistreated. When the mob persisted, the brave Colonel opened fire with a shotgun loaded with squirrel shot. "Three of the rioters were peppered and wounded and the balance of the hoodlums, having regard for their hides, disbanded and the fun was over."

It was reported that only one peace officer made an appearance during the entire evening, and that was not done until most of the trouble had ended. The remainder of the officials were nowhere around, ". . . so that it can be plainly and truthfully said that Sour Lake is without protection from mob violence or any other outrage." It was also noted that the victims had in no way been offensive and, therefore, the outbreak was unjustified.

The following day the aroused citizens convened at one of the local restaurants to decide what action they would take. Resolving that law and order must be restored, they immediately established a provisional government with various committees to assist in bringing about some form of law enforcement. Not only were many of the rioters arrested, but an attack was also launched against the entire lawless element. Several days later it was reported, "The air is somewhat purified by the explosion of last week and out of what seemed bad had undoubtedly come good."

The Negroes and Mexicans did return to Sour Lake but when, months later, there was an indication of another riot, a large group of the white population banded together to prevent any new trouble.

Although lawlessness prevailed in Sour Lake during the boom period, it did not compare to the activities in Batson. In fact, some have said that what the criminal element learned in Sour Lake, it later put in full practice in Batson.

After Spindletop, oil prospectors began searching the flat Gulf Coast terrain for humps where oil and gas seeps or paraffin dirt might be. Since Batson's Prairie lay on a salt dome and fizzed with gas every time it rained, it became a logical site for drilling a well. In 1901, the Libby Oil Company drilled down to seven hundred feet but hit only hot salt water. The hot water cooled the spirits of the prospectors and for a time Batson's Prairie was forgotten.

Judge W.L. Douglas, a well-known lawyer in Beaumont during the early 1900's, has been given credit for discovering oil on Batson's Prairie. It appears that Judge Douglas was out hunting one day on the prairie, barefooted, and stepped into some paraffin dirt. Believing that oil was there, he rushed back to Beaumont with the paraffin still on his feet and showed it to Captain William Wiess and Steve Pipkin who had both previously made money at Spindletop. The result was the formation of the Paraffin Oil Company. A rig was moved onto the prairie and drilling commenced. The three men struck oil with the first well on October 31, 1903. It averaged six hundred barrels of oil a day, and although it could not compare with the hundred thousand barrel Lucas gusher, it was certainly good enough to start another boom.

The story goes that when the well came in, some of the oil sprayed a horse. Its rider, like Paul Revere, rode to nearby Sour Lake to spread the word, and before the horse could turn around, boomers were on their way to Batson. The news spread quickly to Spindletop and Saratoga, where a mass exodus likewise took place.

The "get-rich-quick" rode, waded, and walked through the Thicket, and almost overnight the bald prairie around Batson became the wildest, roughest boom town in Southeast Texas. It soon became a gathering place for the dregs of society, who brought little with them but the essential cards, dice and, of course, the pistols they always wore. Almost all came under aliases such as Indian Joe, Broom Face Jimmy, or The Big Thicket Kid. The nosey soon learned that it was not too wise to ask a stranger his full name because this kind of curiosity was generally not appreciated.

When a gambler one day was supposedly asked by a saloon-keeper what he thought of the town, he seemed to describe the situation well. He replied that while he wouldn't accuse everyone in Batson of being a crook, he would say that every crook was there who could get there.

The very inaccessibility of Batson probably was the prime reason for the lawlessness which prevailed. It was miles away from any town, or railroad, or even any good wagon road. During the early part of the boom, the *Beaumont Journal* noted:

> The roads leading to Batson Prairie will make a person seasick to travel over. They are the poorest sort of apologies for roadways. But it does appear that nothing can stop a man who has oil fever and wishes to reach a new field . . . . People are flocking to the new field in droves. . . . Houses and tents are being pitched overnight, and all the discomforts of living are undergone in the wild rush for fortune. . . . I know of one young fellow — Osceola Archer, formerly of Austin— who cleaned up about $10,000 in a very few hours by buying and selling options at Batson. There are others who have done as well.

A month after the first well came in, one hundred houses lined the main road, Fannin Street. Some of these were general stores, and boarding houses but most were saloons and gambling houses. Many of the establishments never bothered to hang doors because they never had reason to close.

Dr. John Bevil, who practiced medicine in Batson during the boom days, tells a story illustrating the inferior construction of some of the buildings. His office was in the back of a drug store which was bordered on each side by a saloon. Dr. Bevil stated that he was alarmed one day when a gun battle took place in one of the saloons. Every time he and the druggist heard a shot, they both quickly ducked behind a counter because several times a bullet would go astray and come sailing through the almost paper-thin walls.

As more people came, tents appeared between and behind the buildings, and before long they stretched all the way to the oil field, one mile away. In *Tales from the Derrick Floor*, Hardeman Roberts, who arrived in Batson at the height of the boom, relates the precariousness of tent life his first night in the town:

> I walked across there from Sour Lake. There was three of us. . . . We walked to keep from riding on those corduroy roads around there, which would shake you plumb to death. And I got there — we got in there— found a little tent with no floors; had some cots, and right next door to a little flatboard saloon with the gambling house in the back end. I went to bed. All I done was pulled off my shoes. I lay down. I was just dozing off when they started an argument in the gambling house there, and commenced to throwing beer bottles, and started shooting; and about the second shot must have knocked a hat full of dirt from under my cot. So I come out of there.

Before the boom, law enforcement was handled by the county sheriff and one deputy because there had been no need for anything more. But by January, 1904, the population had soared to ten thousand. As the crowd came, crime also increased, and other officials had to be appointed. However, some were not too concerned about maintaining law and order. They, along with many of the businessmen, agreed that fights brought on the crowd, and the crowd brought on the business. With money flowing so freely, the officers and the businessmen felt entitled to a fair share.

The Monday morning "round up," as it came to be called, shows how lawlessness was sanctioned. The "round up" was a way of raising money to pay the salaries of the officials. Each Monday morning the gamblers and prostitutes were arrested for vagrancy and brought before the Justice of the Peace in a courtroom on the second floor of the Crosby House saloon. Usually the procedure was the same in each case. The judge would first ask the culprits their names, reprimand them for their misdeeds and conclude by asking them to show evidence of any visible means of support. Since it was difficult for the gamblers and ladies to show such evidence, the judge would set their fines, which were substantial enough to be divided between him, the arresting officer, and the sheriff's office at Kountze. Then the young women would be paraded out onto the second floor porch below which a jeering crowd of men would be gathered. Someone would yell out the amount of each woman's fine and the first man who made it to court and paid the fine could take the woman home with him for twenty-four hours. It seemed that there was never a shortage of men. However, the job of hauling the women into court each week became so tiring that the madams came instead and paid the fines.

When the "round up" was in use, one or two of the women liked to shock the judge by answering

THE BATSON AUCTION: where women of "light repute" were auctioned off to the highest bidders.

(Courtesy Clyde Gray's Heritage Garden, Woodville, Texas.)

THE BIG CASINO BAR, one of the many Big Thicket saloons during the oil-boom era. (Courtesy Lamar Library - Fisher Collection)

"yes" when asked if they had any visible means of support. Since the judge knew what was coming, he would stop them before they showed any evidence. However, one day the judge was feeling quite jovial and went along with a woman when she replied that she did indeed have visible means of support. "Very well," the official expounded, "Will you please show the court the means of your support or pay a fine of twenty-five dollars and costs." As she proceeded to lift her skirt, the judge hollered, "Never mind, put your dress down." What made the story amusing was not the joke but the appearance of the woman. She was about fifty years old, not over five feet tall, and weighed all of two hundred pounds. Her physique was enhanced by her brown, crossed eyes, large ears, and a mouth filled with buck teeth.

Fights and shootings occurred so frequently that they soon became part of the daily routine. The experiences of Plummer Barfield illustrate the violent activities carried on one winter night in Batson. In 1904, as a boy of no more than thirteen or fourteen, he began working in a livery stable. Plummer slept at the stable at night and was responsible for such varied chores as taking care of the horses and hauling in the wounded, the crippled, and the dead, for in those days the livery stable also served as an undertaking parlor. In recalling the hectic night he stated:

> There was a roughneck killed in the field. . . and I went in the field and loaded the body. Started back to the livery stable and got halfway back, why, I met a bunch of men with lanterns milling around in the road. And they stopped me and asked me what I had, and I told them I had a body. Says, "Well, throw him out. We got some more work for you to do." Well, they drug him out to the side of the

road and left him there. And pointed to a
tent over there that had a light in it and a
bunch of lanterns around it . . . there was
a dead woman and a baby. I loaded them
both up and went on to the livery stable
and unloaded them and put them on what
was known as the "cooling board" in
those days. . . .

About the time I got that done, why, a
couple of roughnecks come in and says,
"When you get time," says, "you'll find
two more." . . .

So I went on back down the road and
picked up the man I'd laid beside the road
at first, and brought him up and put him
in the wagon bed back in the livery
stable. Didn't have no more boards. . . .

. . . I'd learned why there were two more
down there. This lady's baby had taken
sick, and she's got up to give it a dose of
medicine or tend to it, and some rattle-
brain drunks shot at the light, see,
through the tent. . . . And these rough-
necks and rig runners around there, they
caught those two guys and hung them to
a sweetgum tree. And them was the two
men that I went back and got. I cut them
down and hauled them in.

At first when prisoners were arrested, they were
taken immediately to the jail at Kountze. The task
soon became too great, and another system had to
be devised. The officers then started chaining the
prisoners to trees in town until wagons could collect them and haul them to Kountze. It was not un-
common for a prisoner to be chained for as long as
forty-eight hours, subjected not only to the climatic
conditions, but also to the jibes of the passersby.

While women were not exempt from such debas-
ing treatment, their chances of being released were

greater than that of the male prisoners. If a woman had charms enough to persuade a passerby to pay her fine, her charges were dismissed and she was released to his custody. The pair could live together as man and wife on the main street of town, but were refused residence on the field close to the wells where the more respectable citizens lived.

Finally, the lawless element became so rampant that it began to interfere with the work in the oil field. The prosperous "rough-necks" were easy targets for organized gunmen and racketeers in Batson. The outlaws would rob them on the road at night and, if they resisted, they would beat them and often kill them. Numerous bodies were found in shallow graves in the field or in the nearby bayou. Prostitutes who had little or no protection also fell prey to this murdering element.

Out of sheer desperation, leaders of the community called on the Governor to send the Texas Rangers into the town. On February 7, 1904, Captain J.A. Brooks arrived in Batson. With the help of three assistants and the aid of the Good Government League established by some lawful citizens, Captain Brooks began to bring about many of the needed reforms.

By 1908 the boom in the Big Thicket was over. As oil production decreased, the riff-raff and the big time operators moved on to newer fields. Sour Lake, Batson, and Saratoga were left to the few respectable citizens who chose to remain.

CHAPTER IV

The Violent

Era

The 1920's and early 1930's were turbulent years not only in the vicinity of the Big Thicket but throughout the rest of the nation as well. Following World War I Americans were becoming increasingly alarmed over the crime wave which was sweeping the cities. In the South the white population was offended by the more aggressive attitude of the Negro returning from the war or from a job in the North. The supposed shrewdness of the Jew and the alleged dominance of the Catholic Church were also causes of concern. People everywhere were advocating a return to normalcy, a quest for law and order. Their regressive feelings soon were manifested in such ways as participating in lynchings, supporting prohibition, which made a criminal out of anyone who sold or manufactured alcoholic beverages, and joining the revived order of the Ku Klux Klan.

KLAN ACTIVITIES

Texas was particularly receptive to the Klan. Its cities were growing rapidly, and men, concerned over the increased lawlessness, looked to the organization as a means to clean up the community. By the early part of 1921 the Klan had moved into every section of the state and had attracted some of the most prominent men in each community. Reports were made almost daily of masked men making physical attacks on Negroes, bootleggers, unfaithful husbands, and anyone else who violated the Klan's strict code of conduct. Although the Klan was publicly criticized by the press and inves-

93

tigated from time to time by various grand juries, its activities went virtually unchecked until the end of 1923.

Some of the most violent assaults by Klan members were reported to have occurred in Southeast Texas. On the evening of May 7, 1921, a well-known Beaumont physician, Dr. J.S. Paul, was kidnapped from his office by masked men, forced into an automobile and taken into the woods of the nearby Big Thicket. There he was severely beaten and tarred and feathered by the group who admitted that they were members of the Ku Klux Klan. He was subsequently returned to the city and deposited in the heart of the business section.

The following July fifteen masked men set up a roadblock near the town of Orange and forced R.F. Scott, a logger of Deweyville, into a wooded area where he was whipped unmercifully, tarred, feathered, and dropped at the busiest corner in Beaumont.

A few days later the *Beaumont Enterprise* received a letter which bore the seal "knights of the Ku Klux Klan No. 7, Beaumont, Texas" and which supposedly showed justification of the harsh treatment received by Dr. Paul and Mr. Scott. According to the letter, portions of which were published in the newspaper on July 23, Dr. Paul was under indictment for abortion and Mr. Scott was indicted jointly with him. There appeared throughout the letter such comments as: "Wrong rules the land and waiting justice sleeps. . . . The eyes of the unknown had seen and had observed the wrong to be redressed. . . . The law of the Klan is justice."

During the same year, Klan activities rocked the town of Sour Lake when a body of masked men gained admittance into the home of the Justice of the Peace, J.J. De Vere. De Vere was taken into a section south of town where he received the lashing and tar and feather treatment. As to the reason for the punishment, it was speculated that De Vere was guilty of the illegal sale of intoxicants. Warned by the masked men to leave town, the officer immediately departed for Liberty. Rumors soon began circulating in Sour Lake that friends of Judge De Vere were organizing a vigilante committee for the purpose of a vengeful attack on the guilty parties. From what source such attack would come and when it would occur were mere conjectures. Some believed that "anti-klansmen" were organizing forces within the town, while others felt that the invasion would come from Liberty. When it was reported that several prominent men of Sour Lake had received similar threats, many of the citizens of Sour Lake were deputized by the Hardin County sheriff, W.L. Nelson, to fortify the town against attack. The deputies, along with an equal number of other citizens, kept vigil over the town and patrolled the highways leading into the town. After several days the attack failed to materialize, the people began to relax and calm was restored.

Citizens of Liberty were reportedly quite amazed when they heard that they were supposed to have been the invaders. Statements were made later by officials of the town denying the rumors.

> If any emergency should arise that would call upon the citizenship of Liberty to go anywhere, we'd go all right, but we wouldn't go as a gang, or a mob; we wouldn't go masked or hooded and we wouldn't make the time of our arrival at some dark hour in the night . . . . The news that such was the case was a surprise and shock to us. Peace and harmony reign here, and the best of feeling exists between the citizens of the two towns.

The De Vere incident split Sour Lake into two factions for a period of nearly three years. While many of the leading citizens of the community belonged to the Klan, just as many were "anti-klansmen."

Sour Lake was only one example of how Klan activities were disrupting the unity of communities throughout the entire South. By the fall of 1921, the Ku Klux Klan was gaining more strength. Huge parades and rallies were frequently staged by Klansmen and attacks on "wrong-doers" increased. The "invisible order" was anything but unseen.

By the spring of 1922, however, local governments throughout the state began to increase their investigations of the Klan activities, and, as a result, much of the vigilante work of Klansmen was brought to an end. For example, on March 29, the mayor of Beaumont, B.A. Steinhagen, issued the following statement to the public:

> The city commission does not presume to dictate to any employee, or otherwise, as to their affiliation with any organization. We are firmly convinced, however, that it is inimical to the public interest for any employee of the city to be a member of the Ku Klux Klan, and no one a member of such organization will remain in the employ of this city.

In May, 1922, a Jefferson County deputy sheriff, George Wallace, was fined $100 and jailed for his refusal before the grand jury to answer a question relating to his membership in the Ku Klux Klan. In the complaint filed on behalf of the State it was alleged that Mr. Wallace had participated in some of the incidents which had previously occurred in Beaumont in connection with the Klan.

In spite of strong anti-Klan forces, the Ku Klux Klan continued to wield influence in Texas until the end of 1923. Its turn from acting as "judge, jury, and executioner," to its involvement in politics dur-

ing the latter period no doubt contributed more
than any other factor to keeping the membership
active.

RACIAL VIOLENCE

Hostility toward minority groups was not confined to members of the Ku Klux Klan. Many white
Southerners, including residents of the Big Thicket, considered Negroes to be inferior. These Whites
contended that if a Negro "stayed in his place," he
was a "good Nigger;" and if he became "uppity," he
was "bad" and "needed to be dealt with." This belief was particularly predominant among the older
whites and those living in rural communities.

Throughout the history of the Big Thicket, white
citizens were accustomed to acting outside the
realm of the law. This was especially true when a
Negro was thought to be involved in a crime. Then
they acted quickly. Race riots, such as the one previously mentioned in Sour Lake, had occurred periodically, but never had sentiment toward the
Negro race been as adverse as it was during the
years following World War I. Although lynchings
and racial disorders were frequently taking place
throughout the country, they were more prevalent
in the South.

The following incidents which occurred in the Big
Thicket area are only two examples of how many
people during the period were prone to become
fanatical and tended to lose all sense of justice.

At the same time that Sour Lake was experienc-
ing trouble with the Ku Klux Klan, the first reported lynching took place in the town. On November
26, 1921, a Negro storekeeper, Henry Cade, who had
been accused of criminally assaulting a white girl,
was hanged outside of town by a mob of irate citizens.

The incident stemmed from the report that earlier in the day an eight-year-old girl, Cleo Colter,
had gone to Cade's grocery store on an errand for

97

her mother. Upon her return, the girl told her parents that she was ill and went to bed. Later, fearing that the child's condition might be serious, the parents called a physician to examine her. It was then that the girl told the story of the attack. The father of the child immediately went to the store and fired twice at Cade, hitting him in the face and abdomen. Two deputy sheriffs reached the store, disarmed the girl's father, and placed the seriously wounded Negro in an automobile in an endeavor to take him to the county jail in Kountze for safekeeping. However, by that time, news of the attack had spread to all parts of town. A posse of three hundred men overtook the car, dragged Cade from the officers, and stood him on an old road tractor. While a rope was being placed around his neck, the victim protested repeatedly that he was innocent of the crime. Upon an appeal from the deputies, the little girl was brought to the scene. She looked up, pointed her finger at the Negro on the make-shift gallows, and stated, "He's the man." Five seconds later the Negro was hanged.

The reactions of some Hardin County residents were even more violent in December, 1933. Mrs. Mellie W. Brockman, a young mother of three, was en route to town when she was attacked and slain on the afternoon of December 3, in a lonely section of woods close to Kountze. The alleged killer was reported also to have set fire to her truck. Her partially-burned body was later found by members of the Civilian Conservation Corps who had gone to check on the fire. After officers were notified and an investigation was conducted, three Negroes were arrested and questioned about the murder. While the Negroes were not believed to be suspects themselves, it was reported that they possessed information pertinent to the case.

On December 5, David Gregory, a twenty-four-year-old Negro and an ex-convict, was formally charged with the assault and murder of Mrs. Brockman. Rewards totaling $700 were posted for his capture, and the search, which was already underway, turned into one of the most intensive manhunts ever conducted in the area. Hardin County officers received a tip that a strange Negro fitting the description of Gregory had been seen in Voth, a small town south of Kountze. Miles Jordan, the sheriff of Hardin County, along with Deputy Ralph Chance, hurried to Voth, where they were met by officers of Jefferson County, Sheriff W.W. "Bill" Richardson and Deputy Homer French. Together they proceeded to the yard of the Mount Zion Baptist Church, the place where Gregory was believed to be hiding. As the officers advanced toward the church, a young Negro boy ran toward them exclaiming, "He's in here," and pointed to the belfrey of the church. Ordered to surrender, Gregory refused and threatened to shoot. Shots from the gun of Deputy Chance answered his defiance. The discharge struck Gregory in the right side of the head, shooting out his right eye and tearing away part of his neck. Sheriffs Jordan and Richardson then climbed into the belfrey and lowered the Negro to the ground. They placed Gregory in an automobile and rushed him to Hotel Dieu Hospital in Beaumont, where the officers waited at his bedside hoping doctors could revive him long enough to obtain a confession.

At the hospital, Sheriff Jordan received various telephone calls stating that a mob from Hardin County was en route to Beaumont to take the Negro. Fearful of violence, the officers placed Gregory back in the automobile and headed toward the town of Orange. Soon after leaving Beaumont, Gregory died. The officers then went to Silsbee, where they planned to place the body in a funeral home. When they arrived, a crowd stopped the automobile and demanded the Negro's body. However, Sheriff Jordan made a strong appeal against violence and the officers were allowed to go on to

MILES JORDAN, sheriff of Hardin County in the 1930's and early 1940's, who successfully tracked down Big Thicket fugitives, David Gregory and "Red" Goleman.

Kountze.

An account by Sheriff Jordan vividly relates the events which followed.

> As I entered Kountze, I saw a large crowd blocking my way. It was just a sea of silent, but grimly determined men. I suppose I might have got part of the way through by running over and killing a bunch of white men, but I would not do that for a dead negro. I tried to get them to listen to reason but they would not. They quickly dragged the body from my automobile. I could do nothing against 400 men.

The mob threw Gregory's body to the ground and placed a chain under his arms and tied it to the back of a car. It was then dragged through the streets of the Negro section of the town, followed by the angry mob whose members were armed with knives and pistols.

The gory procession lasted for over an hour. At intervals the car would stop and the avengers would attack the body, horribly mutilating it. Finally after the heart had been carved out of the body, someone suggested that the body be burned. Lumber was immediately piled along the side of a Negro street and a fire lighted. The climax did not come, however, until the remains were forceably shown to Gregory's mother. The body was then flung into the roaring fire.

Throughout the next day, people could be seen poking in the still smoldering ashes of the funeral pyre, searching for small pieces of human bones which were the only relics that remained of the lynching. These were either saved or traded as souvenirs, some of which are still around today to remind people of how justice was administered in 1933.

MOUNT ZION BAPTIST Church in Voth, where officers
of Hardin and Jefferson counties shot David Gregory
who was hiding in the church belfrey.

SITE WHERE AN irate Kountze mob burned the body of
David Gregory in December, 1933.

There were no verified lynchings nor any reported racial strife in the Thicket town of Saratoga after World War I. The Blacks were just not allowed
there. Some people say that the Negroes were driv-
en out in the early part of the twentieth century after a white girl was criminally assaulted by a black
man. For many years, posted at each side of town,
were identical signs reading, "Black man, don't let
the sun set on you in Saratoga." During the busy
oil producing days, the oil companies often employed Blacks as mule skinners who drove mule-
drawn wagons which hauled pipe and drilling
machinery from the T. & N.O. Railroad at Nome or
from one oil field to another. However, black driv-
ers were replaced by whites at Batson because the
next stop was Saratoga.

Around the year 1921, feelings against Blacks
were emphasized by the following two incidents.
One story is told about a Negro, apparently from
another part of the State or country, who got off the
train in Saratoga and started walking down the
board sidewalk of the town with his coat thrown
nonchalantly over his shoulder. The men on the
street moved close together and stood watching the
stranger for a moment, then without saying anything, charged at him simultaneously. One man in
front caught him by the arm, but the Negro was
able to break away and outdistanced his pursuers.
When last seen, he was running at top speed into
the dense protection of the Thicket.

The second story tells of two other unsuspecting
Negroes who left the train in Saratoga, approached
a group of white men, and asked for directions to
the Negro quarters. The group began to laugh and
one of the men pointed to a huge oak tree nearby
where a rope was dangling from one of its branch-
es. "There it is!" he shouted. The two Blacks looked
wide-eyed at each other, turned quickly, and started running toward the train depot. In spite of the
distance, the white men could hear what the Ne-

groes were saying. "I thinks we better catch de next train out of here!" one of them hollered. "Naw, Suh!" the other one yelled, "I'm gittin on dat one dat jist left!"

REPRODUCTIONS OF A picture and a story on the back given to the author in 1962 by the late Deputy Sheriff Edward Gary, Jefferson County Sheriff's Department. However, nothing was found to verify that a multiple hanging occurred in Saratoga, Texas, in 1909. A similar incident did take place during a race riot in Sabine County in June, 1908. The story can be found in the *Beaumont Journal,* June 23, 1908, page 3.

"A family group"
"Just hanging around"
Saratoga, Texas - 1909

A white young girl was criminally assaulted by one of these bro-thers. The posse killed three negroes they just happened to run into in woods and on road. The one chased by dogs killed one De-puty - the dogs chased him to his home. None of the brothers would tell who assaulted the girl so they hung them all to be sure the right one was hung.

105

THOMAS "White Eyes" Williford (center) was appointed sheriff of Hardin County in 1918 after the death of W.C. "Clark" Jordan. People who can remember Williford never fail to mention that he performed the last legal execution in Hardin County. (Of course, there were several not so legal ones to follow.) On July 8, 1918, James Franklin, a Negro accused of murdering his wife, was sentenced to be hanged the following week on Friday, August 16. People came from all over the Thicket to witness the execution and before the day was over, it turned into one of the most celebrated affairs in the history of Hardin County.

(Courtesy Sheriff Billy Payne, Kountze, Texas.)

CHAPTER V

East Texas
Desperado

For years the illegal making of whiskey has been a way of life and income for some residents of the Big Thicket. As early as 1915, the *Hardin County Herald* reported that bootlegging led all other crimes in the area. But it was particularly during the days of national prohibition that the practice became most apparent. The setting of the Thicket was ideal for bootlegging. However, many persons stirred up their "brew" only to have it confiscated by the revenue officers and the makers arrested. In spite of these arrests, bootlegging continued throughout the period and even today stills are occasionally found.

Only recently when Billy Paine, Hardin County sheriff, was told about an active still, he quickly set out to confiscate it. Thinking that he would have to search a long time because the offender lived in the deepest part of the Big Thicket, Sheriff Paine was surprised to find the still in full view in the man's front yard. It appeared that it was a little too much trouble for the "brew-maker" to check his recipe each day in the dense woods which surrounded his house. While the moonshiner did not seem to mind paying his fine, his big complaint was that he was trying a new recipe and would never know if it had been a good one.

One moonshiner of the 1930's was Thomas Jefferson "Red" Goleman, who grew his corn and operated his still at the edge of the Big Thicket on Pine Island Bayou. However, "Red" was not satisfied with such trivial lawbreaking and went on to big time crimes, winning for himself the title of "Texas Public Enemy No. 1."

Goleman spent most of his early life in the Big Thicket around the Little Rock settlement between Kountze and Sour Lake. His mother was known to be a hard working woman who helped make a living for her family by washing and ironing for neighbors. The father moved from one place to another doing various odd jobs. Although as a boy "Red" had some minor encounters with the law, many people did not label him as "bad" and remembered him as being quite industrious.

When "Red" was grown, his behavior grew increasingly worse, and he was frequently involved in some sort of wrong-doing. Working as a rig builder in the East Texas oil fields, he gained the reputation of being a brawler. His fights generally occurred after each pay day and invariably resulted in his arrest. As the steel rig supplanted the old wooden type, Goleman moved away and was unheard of for several years.

Allegedly, his first major criminal offense was committed in Corpus Christi, where he was charged with the murder of one of his few close acquaintances, C.W. "Four Eyes" Brown, who was later found floating in the Nueces River. After Goleman's arrest, he was released on bond but failed to appear when his case was set for trial. He dropped out of sight until three months later when he appeared in East Texas in the sedate little town of Hull on the western edge of the Big Thicket, and added another black mark to his record, the robbery of the Hull State Bank.

Hazel Hilliard, an employee of the bank, recalled this incident as probably the most startling experience of her life, and no doubt the most talked about incident ever to occur in Hull. When "Red" Goleman and his companion, Francis Elva Smith, robbed the Hull State Bank, Miss Hilliard and Florine Hudnall, another employee of the bank were

THOMAS JEFFERSON "Red" Goleman (above) was the most
notorious Big Thicket outlaw of the 1930's. After robbing the
Hull State Bank, he evaded capture for several months by hiding
out in the Thicket, living on the varied wild-life and provisions
smuggled to him by some of the old nesters of the area.

(Picture appeared in the *Beaumont Enterprise,* April 12, 1940.)

109

alone at noontime on July 26, 1939. The two masked bandits walked into the bank and, with pistols drawn, ordered the two terrified women into the vault, then commanded Miss Hilliard to open the safe. After sacking the money, which amounted to $12,000 in cash, the armed robbers locked the women in the vault, leaped into a waiting sedan, and quickly drove away. Moments later a male customer entered the bank and noticing no one there, remarked, "Where is everybody? This would be an ideal time for a bank robbery." When the women heard his voice, they began pounding on the door of the vault and screaming for help. The man was able to open the vault door and soon released the women.

The three reported the robbery; roadblocks were quickly set up, and police were alerted all over East Texas. The search was not a long one, for several days later Goleman was turned over to the Hardin county sheriff, Miles Jordan, by Goleman's kinsmen. He was then taken to Liberty County, the county where the robbery occurred, and jailed. Goleman readily confessed to the crime and agreed to return what was left of his share of the money, but refused to divulge the name of his accomplice. After a delay of two days as a result of Goleman's attempt to commit suicide by slashing his arm with a tobacco tin, Goleman led officers to a remote spot in the Big Thicket, where he unearthed a fruit jar containing $645 of the missing money. A smaller portion was later found buried in Houston.

The second suspect, Francis Elva Smith, was arrested shoftly after, and legal proceedings began. Smith retained Percy Foreman of Houston to represent him, but Goleman refused to hire counsel, stating, "I am going to face the music like a man." He was subsequently represented by counsel appointed by the court. The suspects were released on $6,000 bond each, but failed to appear when their cases were called. Although Smith was soon apprehended in Kansas City, Missouri, Goleman remained at large for several months. Once more, the Big Thicket, the land which he knew so well, became his home.

During these months East Texas residents were terrified. To them "Red" Goleman turned loose in the Thicket could be compared to "Jack-the-Ripper" roaming the streets of London. Hunters were even apprehensive. Goleman was familiar with every path and trail, and with the help of many of the old nesters, some of whom were his relatives, he was easily able to avoid capture. On several occasions Hardin County officers ventured into the dense forest with hounds and other methods of tracking but were never successful in finding the outlaw. Once the officers were within a few feet of Goleman, but he threw them off by wading through miles of swamp water. Living like a wild beast, the fugitive fed on berries, nuts, and roots which the forest generously provided.

One day officers went to the home of Goleman's grandmother, who lived in the Little Rock settlement, and questioned her about her grandson's whereabouts. As she emphatically denied knowing anything about Goleman, he lay in the attic and listened intently to the conversation taking place below.

It seemed that he could pop up from out of nowhere, commit a crime, and return to the Thicket without leaving a trace. A story is told about "Red" stepping from behind a tree one day onto the running board of a passing car near Kirbyville, Texas. The startled driver, looking into the muzzle of a loaded gun, was ordered to stop his car and get into the trunk. With the intention of robbing and killing the man, the fugitive drove directly to one of his hiding places in the Thicket. However, after releasing his captive from the trunk, Goleman changed his mind. By his wits alone, the terrified man was able to gain "Red's" confidence. He convinced the desperado that he needed money also and wanted to become his partner in crime. He told Goleman about a bank in Dayton, Texas, with a large amount of money that he had been watching for a long time. The outlaw and his new-found friend spent the remainder of the day making detailed plans to rob the Dayton bank.

The captured man was able to leave the following afternoon under the pretense of going to his home to prepare for the event. He and Goleman made an appointment to meet two nights later on the railroad tracks one mile west of Dayton. The man immediately contacted, W.W. "Bill" Richardson, the sheriff of Jefferson County. Richardson had the reputation of being very successful in capturing criminals, and he alerted officials in Liberty County where the proposed crime was scheduled to take place. Two nights later, the released captive walked down the railroad tracks near Dayton to keep his promised rendezvous while highway patrolmen, sheriff's deputies, and armed volunteers, were hidden along the tracks. For several hours, the men anxiously waited for Goleman to appear. Their vigil was in vain, however, for Goleman, apparently, had grown suspicious and failed to appear.

On January 8, 1940, Goleman, along with his younger brother, Darious, allegedly shot, robbed, and brutally beat a Beaumont taxi driver by the name of Charles Lockley. A surveying crew found the cab several weeks later parked in some dense undergrowth near Kountze.

By March, Texas' No. 1 desperado had been charged with numerous other robberies and kidnappings, even some which he did not commit. Rumors circulated practically every day as to his whereabouts. One report was that Goleman had been seen swimming in the Neches River, while another alleged that he had been killed in Nacogdoches, Texas.

For several weeks, Jefferson and Hardin County

officers, determined to bring an end to Goleman's crimes, quietly kept vigil at several strategic points. Every known friend of the bandit, every relative was watched. Finally, the officers felt encouraged that they might be on the right track when a deputy, who had trailed Goleman's mother for several days, saw her buy overalls, buckshot shells, and a large supply of groceries at the Kirby Lumber Company Commissary in Voth, Texas. The officers had also been contacted by a reliable source telling them where the outlaw was supposed to be hiding.

Believing that Goleman meant his boast that he would not surrender, the officers were fully prepared to capture him, whatever the cost. On the afternoon of April 11, a posse was formed which included Sheriff Richardson and his chief deputies, Homer French, Edgar Pool, J. Howard "Pistol" Allen, Sheriff Miles Jordan of Kountze, and Highway Patrolman Charlie Meyers. That afternoon these officers watched the farmhouse which belonged to Goleman's grandmother and where the desperado was reported to be. They waited in silence for several hours, then, finally late in the night they noticed the grandmother leave a small shed in the rear of the farmhouse. They observed a dim light burning in the building. As the officers moved in, the light went out. One officer, Deputy Allen, entered the farmhouse where he found the startled grandmother, along with the outlaw's mother, a sister and a brother-in-law. As Allen guarded these relatives, the other lawmen surrounded the crude shed which had several wide cracks between its rough boards. One deputy turned on a flashlight and the officers could see a reflection from Goleman's pistol. Knowing that he stood huddled in one corner of the building, they called out to him to surrender, but the outlaw fired his gun in defiance. The posse returned the fire, riddling the shed and the bandit with bullets. When they heard Goleman cry out, they cautiously approached the house where they found him dead from numerous bullet wounds. The crumpled body was clad in the new denim overalls, and, pushed against the shed wall, stood the yet unopened sack of groceries and a bedroll. Goleman apparently was headed for a new hide-out deep in the Big Thicket. As one account aptly put it, "Finis was written to another 'bad man' who believed he could beat the law."

Goleman may have spent his last days alone in the Thicket but at the instant of his death, his body became anything but private property. He was photographed from almost every angle both at his last Thicket hideout and in the Beaumont mortuary where the body was taken. A can of abrasive cleanser is shown in one photograph which was necessary to cleanse the mud-stained body. In another photograph thick callouses are obvious on the soles of the outlaw's feet.

Thomas Jefferson "Red" Goleman was buried in the Old Hardin Cemetery not many miles from the spot where he was born and where he was killed. The funeral was described as the biggest one ever held in Hardin County. People came from all over East Texas and the western part of Louisiana. Some cars were spotted from Missouri, Mississippi, Oklahoma, and several other states. The long service, which consisted of sermons from four preachers and several songs sung by a choir, became so emotional that several fainted and many women became hysterical. For almost an hour the crowd, estimated at nearly four thousand persons, filed by the casket to get their final curious glimpse of the man who for so long had terrorized the area. When the time came to close the casket, many, believing that they would not get to view the body, began to push and shove and for a short time officers were needed to control the confusion.

All was not over when the funeral ended. For the price of only ten cents, charged by the Goleman family, hundreds were able to witness for themselves the spot where the famous outlaw shot it out to the bitter end.

AFTER "Red" GOLEMAN was buried in the Old Hardin Cemetery, hundreds of people drove to the spot where he was killed. The picture on the right shows the outlaw's shoes and other items found in the old shed.

(Courtesy Lamar Library - Fisher Collection.)

115

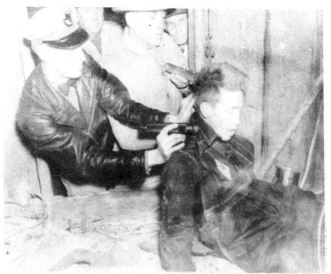

"RED" OFTEN BOASTED that he would not surrender, so when Hardin and Jefferson County officers trailed him to a small shed in the rear of a farmhouse, they did not hesitate to riddle him with bullets. After he was killed, numerous pictures were taken. In the second photograph, his body is surrounded by Hardin and Jefferson County officers.

(Courtesy Mrs. Homer French, Beaumont, Texas.)

CHAPTER VI

Death's Duo

in the Thicket

As the body of "Red" Goleman lay in a Beaumont mortuary awaiting burial, Darious Goleman was confined in the Jefferson County jail on the charge of assisting in the robbery and assault of the cab driver, Charles Lockley. Darious was not allowed to attend his brother's funeral, but on request of his grandmother, he was granted permission to go to the funeral home. While he was viewing the corpse, his grandmother was reported to have told Darious that if he did not change his ways, he, too, would earn for himself a similar death. Darious did not follow her advice, for he chose to follow the path of his ill-fated brother and likewise paid the highest price, his life, as his debt to society.

Darious was convicted of the charges that he was under for robbery and assault and was sentenced to the state penitentiary for ten years. While he was in prison, he met and became friends with a former Beaumont truck driver, Alex Leviness, who was serving sentence on a similar offense. After several years both men were released from prison and presumably went their separate ways.

In June, 1949, however, the two were arrested as suspects for the murder of a Beaumont housewife, Mrs. Eloise Twitchell. They were subsequently indicted by the grand jury of Hardin County where the alleged murder occurred, and separate trials were scheduled. Believing that fair trials could not be obtained in Hardin County, Houston Thompson, one of the attorneys for the accused, applied for a change of venue. Thompson stated that the news media had so influenced local people that a

ALEX LEVINESS (second from left) and Darious Goleman (second from right) are pictured with Hardin county officers shortly after their arrest in June, 1949.

fair trial could not be held in the county. Particularly in the case of Darious Goleman, the affidavit stated that prejudice existed against him because of the past records of some of his relatives. In addition to the reputation established by his brother, Thomas Jefferson "Red" Goleman, two uncles had been convicted of murders in Hardin County. The requests were denied. Leviness was tried in July, 1949, and the trial of Goleman took place the following September before the seventy-fifth Judicial District Court in Kountze.

Basing most of its evidence on signed confessions from the two defendants, the State presented a strong case in each trial. In his confession Goleman admitted that he and Leviness had planned to rob the Hull State Bank at Hull and had purchased a .38 calibre pistol in Beaumont on September 27, 1948. Goleman stated that the next day, while hitch-hiking, they were offered a ride by Mrs. Twitchell just outside the Beaumont city limits on the Beaumont-Woodville highway. The statement read that Mrs. Twitchell did not become suspicious until they approached the intersection of the Honey Island road with the Woodville highway north of Kountze. Goleman and Leviness asked her to let them out of the car at the intersection and when they got out, she attempted to drive off. Goleman said that it was then that he got back into the car, pointed the gun at her and forced her to stop the car. He said that they had planned to take her so far back into the woods that she would not be able to walk out and report them before they had time to rob the Hull bank. After driving off the highway approximately one hundred yards, Goleman said that the car bogged down in mud. At this point Mrs. Twitchell tried again to escape. Goleman fired two shots at her, but said that he did not know whether she had been injured by them. He declared that the pistol then jammed and Mrs. Twitchell wrested the gun from his hand. According to Gole-

GOLEMAN AND LEVINESS were charged with the murder of
Mrs. Eloise Twitchell

man's statement, Leviness, who was standing behind Mrs. Twitchell, picked up the gun and beat her over the head until she fell to the ground. After this, Goleman stated that he carried the woman into the Thicket. As he started to leave, he noticed that she was still moving, so he took the pistol which he had taken from Leviness and beat her over the head two or three more times before the barrel of the gun broke. In his statement Goleman admitted he then hid the gun and the two men drove to Houston where they abandoned the car and spent the night with Goleman's sister. In conclusion, he stated that he and Leviness parted the following day. Goleman went to Hillister, Texas, where he got a job and later married. Leviness, in his signed confession, admitted participating in the killing, but denied that he had ever handled the pistol. He contended that it was Goleman who pulled the trigger then beat Mrs. Twitchell to death.

Alex Leviness refused to testify in his own behalf at his trial. During Goleman's trial, Goleman repeatedly denied that he had participated in the murder of Mrs. Twitchell or that he had ever known her. He tried to repudiate his written confession declaring that it had been made under duress after officers beat him, cursed him, and threatened his life. He further contended that the confession had been taken a week after he had been arrested, during which time he had not been allowed to consult with an attorney or to see his family in private conference. Nevertheless, the jury found both Goleman and Leviness guilty as charged and assessed their punishments as death in the electric chair.

Both cases were appealed to the Court of Criminal Appeals in Austin, which reversed the death penalty of the two men on the grounds that both had been illegally indicted by a grand jury whose term had expired under a new state statute.

In February of 1950 Goleman attempted to escape from the Hardin County jail by sawing his way out with a hacksaw rumored to have been slipped to him by a sister. He was immediately transferred to the Jefferson County jail for safe-keeping while he awaited his second trial.

Leviness was tried the second time in Anahuac, county seat of Chambers County, in the early part of 1951. He addressed the jury during the defense summation, denying his guilt and begging for his life. He was given life in prison on February 2, 1951. The press reported that the evidence presented in the case was secondary in importance to the exhibition of personalities displayed among the legal counselors. The defense attorney, Houston Thompson, had to be continually reprimanded by the judge and charged to refrain from his overly dramatic behavior in the courtroom. His constant attempt to antagonize the prosecution was successful. On the fourth day of the trial, tempers reached their peak and a physical encounter resulted between Liberty County District Attorney, C.B. Cain, and Attorney Thompson. Thompson, holding a handkerchief over his face, claimed that Cain struck him in the mouth. Cain denied hitting Thompson in the mouth, but admitted striking him in the chest because he lost his temper when Thompson blew cigarette smoke in his face. Thompson admitted later that he had been trying to provoke Cain into physically assaulting him all week because he felt that the incident would give him grounds for reversal of the case. However, both Thompson and Leviness accepted the life sentence and the case was not appealed.

After serving approximately twenty years of his life sentence, Alex Leviness was released from prison and returned to the area of the Big Thicket to start life over. Now married and recently retired from the position of foreman at Kirby Lumber Company in Silsbee, he has apparently made a satisfactory adjustment to his new role of freedom.

Goleman was retried in Liberty, county seat of

Liberty County, and again received the death sentence on April 14, 1951. He heard the verdict with a smile on his face and a cigarette held casually between his teeth. His case was appealed all the way to the United States Supreme Court, which, after much study, failed to intervene. Goleman was sentenced to die on December 4, 1952, but was given the customary thirty-day reprieve by Governor Allen Shivers. Through the efforts of his attorneys, the pardon board granted him a new hearing and an additional reprieve. During the hearing, a request was made to have his sentence changed to life in prison but the request was denied. Finally, on February 4, 1953, time ran out for Darious Goleman. At midnight he walked out of his death cell and into the death chamber unassisted and apparently unafraid. The electric current was applied at 12:05 a.m. and at 12:08 Goleman was pronounced dead.

Goleman claimed his innocence up to the end. In an interview with a prison reporter the day before his death, Goleman stated that officers connected with the case had beaten a confession out of him and that he had been convicted on his previous criminal record. He swore that he would not forgive officers in the case "for murdering me. I just cannot get religious enough to forgive them." He contended, however, that he was not afraid to die but only regretted the circumstances for his mother's sake.

* * * * *

While acts of lawlessness have continued in the Big Thicket since the days of Darious Goleman and Alex Leviness, and will always exist as in any other geographical area, these two outlaws are regarded as among the last notorious criminals from the Big Thicket. Even when considering the more recent brutal slayings of Kountze antique-dealer, Mrs. Mabel McCormick, and her three-year-old grand-daughter, Leslie Bowman, one cannot connect their accused killers, Dennis Ray Anderson and Fred Young, with the Big Thicket. The criminals were outsiders, not products of the Thicket. The murders took place in Kountze because this was where the antiques were that the two men wanted.

Since the days of Goleman and Leviness and the outlaws who preceded them, industrialization has changed the Big Thicket as it has changed the other more remote areas of our country. Modern technology now discourages the criminal from using the seclusion he was once afforded in the area. The moonshiner and the poacher are still in the Thicket but they are running into more obstacles than they did in former years.

Although the outside world is closing in on the area at a rapid rate, the heart of the Big Thicket still remains undisturbed. If a person so desires, he can venture into this remaining wilderness and experience for himself the type of solitude it holds. Among the dense vegetation, he can easily imagine how in the past the Thicket provided the criminal element, both natives and outsiders, with the sanctuary they desired.

We cannot escape the fact that while civilization has destroyed much of the physical characteristics of the Big Thicket, one thing it cannot take away, at least within this generation, is the individualism which exists among some of its people. As far as law and order is concerned, they, like their ancestors before them, are still inclined to take the law and its interpretations, as well as its enforcement, into their own hands.

Shortly after Dennis Ray Anderson and Fred Young were arrested in the McCormick and Bowman murders, Sheriff Billy Paine jokingly asked the accused if they would like to be taken to a local restaurant for dinner. Taking the sheriff quite seriously, the pair immediately began pleading with him not to let them out of their well-fortified cells.

They were completely aware of the temper of the people, knowing quite well that lynch law would prevail just as it had in the past with few words of protest from those outside the jail walls.

DENNIS RAY ANDERSON (front) and Fred Young, accused slayers of antique-dealer Mrs. Mabel McCormick and her granddaughter, Leslie Bowman, are shown soon after their arrest. Although they are not regarded as Big Thicket outlaws, their alleged crimes occurred in the area.

(Courtesy Sheriff Billy Payne, Kountze, Texas.)

A CYPRESS grove at low water

(Roy Hamric - photographer)

THE LAST WITNESS

We stood on unhallowed ground
Deep in Big Thicket
Surrounded by timbers tall;
Once a pioneer had felled the trees
And built a cabin here;
Now there was nothing at all . . .
Only a chimney chinked with clay
Standing a silent watch.

The hunters called it The Graveyard.
They showed us a spot where a woman was killed—
Shot in the back!

There were two men at the hearing
Who had trailed a deer almost to the clearing—
A stag with a crumpled horn.
They swore they heard a rifle whir-r
And saw the woman fall . . .
Her husband came running with a gun . . .
That was all.
The husband claimed that he aimed at the deer
And he was cleared of the crime.

A year went by from the time of the trial
And the two men disappeared.
They were nowhere to be found
Until a guide with a pack of hounds
Came upon them in a gulch . . .
They were covered with limbs and mulch.

Some wagon tracks led from the pioneer shack,
And the man was brought back and tried.
His guilt was anybody's guess,
But he was convicted and sent to the pen;
He never did confess.

The guide had gone with the dogs at dawn,
The hunters had gone to their stands;
John stayed with me but he loaded his gun,
He said sometimes the deer would run by the old place
Instead of down the log trams.

I cringed at the bark of the far-away hounds
as they picked up the scent.
There was death in the air;
There was death in this ground!

I felt a twinge of fear
As I walked to the place where the woman fell,
And I heard the whir-r of a rifle shell,
And the thud of a body on the path.
I caught my breath and held my head
And John came running with his gun . . .
An old, old stag with a crumpled horn
Lay dead!

Was this the last witness, do you suppose?
Only the old, old chimney knows.

Carlyse Bliss
Beaumont, Texas

THE HUNTED AND THE HAUNTED

A cottonmouth comes, sliding wrinkles through
the stillness of the dense black-water slough
and disappears as though he'd never been.
Lean rat with desperate eyes climbs from the bog
and scrambles underneath a crumbled log,
then lies in wait, and sees but is not seen.

Beyond the yaupon and the ancient pine,
beyond palmetto webbed with thorny vine
of briers and brambles woven without wicket,
the hunted and the haunted come to hide,
to creep the devious pathways deep inside
and lose themselves again in the Big Thicket.

The place is still. Whoever enters here
hears only leaf-fall, yet he senses fear,
as if someone is always watching him,
as if a sudden shotgun on the air
could drop a stranger in that tangled lair
where vultures circle, circle, looking grim.

Now, dogtooth violet springs among the stones,
verbena, spiderwort are shielding bones
long hidden in the rotting, mottled leaves.
Last wilderness to screen the nesters' den,
last refuge for the violence of men—
into the brambles every legend weaves.

Violette Newton,
Poet Laureate of Texas, 1973-74